HISTORY'S HEROINES

History's Heroines

Written by Heidi Wirth
Illustrated by Corryn Webb

ALPHECCA BOOKS

Published by Alphecca Books

ALPHECCA BOOKS

www.alpheccabooks.com

Published 2025 in Great Britain

© Heidi Wirth

All rights reserved. No part of this publication may be reproduced, stored in a retrieval system, or transmitted in any form or by any means without the prior written permission of the publisher, except for the use of brief quotations.

ISBN: 978-1-7395936-2-9

Written by Heidi Wirth.

Illustrations and cover illustration by Corryn Webb

Cover formatting, cartography and page embellishments: Richard Tucker

The moral right of Heidi Wirth to be identified as the author this work has been asserted in accordance with the Copyright, Designs and Patents Act 1988

For Sophie and Hunter
Who inspire me every day

Contents

Introduction	1
Timeline	2
Enheduanna	5
Hatshepsut	10
Fu Hao	14
Sammuramat	18
Sappho	22
Telesilla	26
Hydna	30
Artemisia I	34
Artemisia II	38
Cleopatra VII	42
Amanirenas	47
The Trung Sisters	51
Boudicca	55
Zenobia	60
Hypatia	64
Al-Khansa	68
Wu Zetian	72
Aethelflaed	76
Hroswitha	81

FREYDIS EIRIKSDOTTIR	84
MURASAKI SHIKIBU	88
EMMA OF NORMANDY	92
GWENLLIAN FERCH GRUFFYDD	97
TOMOE GOZEN	101
KHUTULUN	105
JULIAN OF NORWICH	109
CHRISTINE DE PIZAN	113
SAYYIDA AL-HURRA	117
HWANG JINI	121
GRACE O'MALLEY	124
AMINA OF ZAZZAU	128
NUR JAHAN	131
NJINGA	134
JAHANARA BEGUM	138
ANNE BONNY	142
MARY READ	146
NG MUI	149
ZHENG YI SAO	153
WANG CONG'ER	157
LOZEN	161
NAKANO TAKEKO	165
FUN QUIZ!	169

Introduction

History is full of famous men – kings, generals, war leaders, politicians, and heroes. But it is not just men who have shaped history – girls and women have been influential, too. There have been many women who have defied the rules of their times. Women who took hold of their lives and forged their own destinies, changing the world in which they lived.

There are books that tell the stories of modern, pioneering women and of mighty queens. But my favourite stories? I like the tales of women from long ago, hundreds and even thousands of years back. If you look hard enough, you can find these women glimmering in the footnotes of our written histories, right back to the early days, the ancient days. So, in these pages you will find women who lived from thousands of years in the past – in the 'B.C.E' (Before Common Era) days – all the way through to more modern times. And they are spread all over the world, too – Europe, Africa, the Middle East, and beyond.

I hope you enjoy this journey through time and around the globe, as you get ready to meet... History's Heroines.

Note:

This book starts thousands of years in the past and moves forward century by century. You will see the dates have 'B.C.E.' or 'C.E.' alongside many of them. Here's a guide to what these abbreviations mean:

B.C.E. – 'Before Common Era', which is over 2,000 years ago. The numbers count backward from year 1. For example, '500 B.C.E.' means 2,500 years ago (2,000 years plus 500 years).

C.E. – 'Common Era', which is the time from 2,000 years ago up to today. It starts at year 1 and counts forward. So '100 C.E.' means 100 years less than 2,000 years ago, i.e. 1,900 years ago.

Timeline

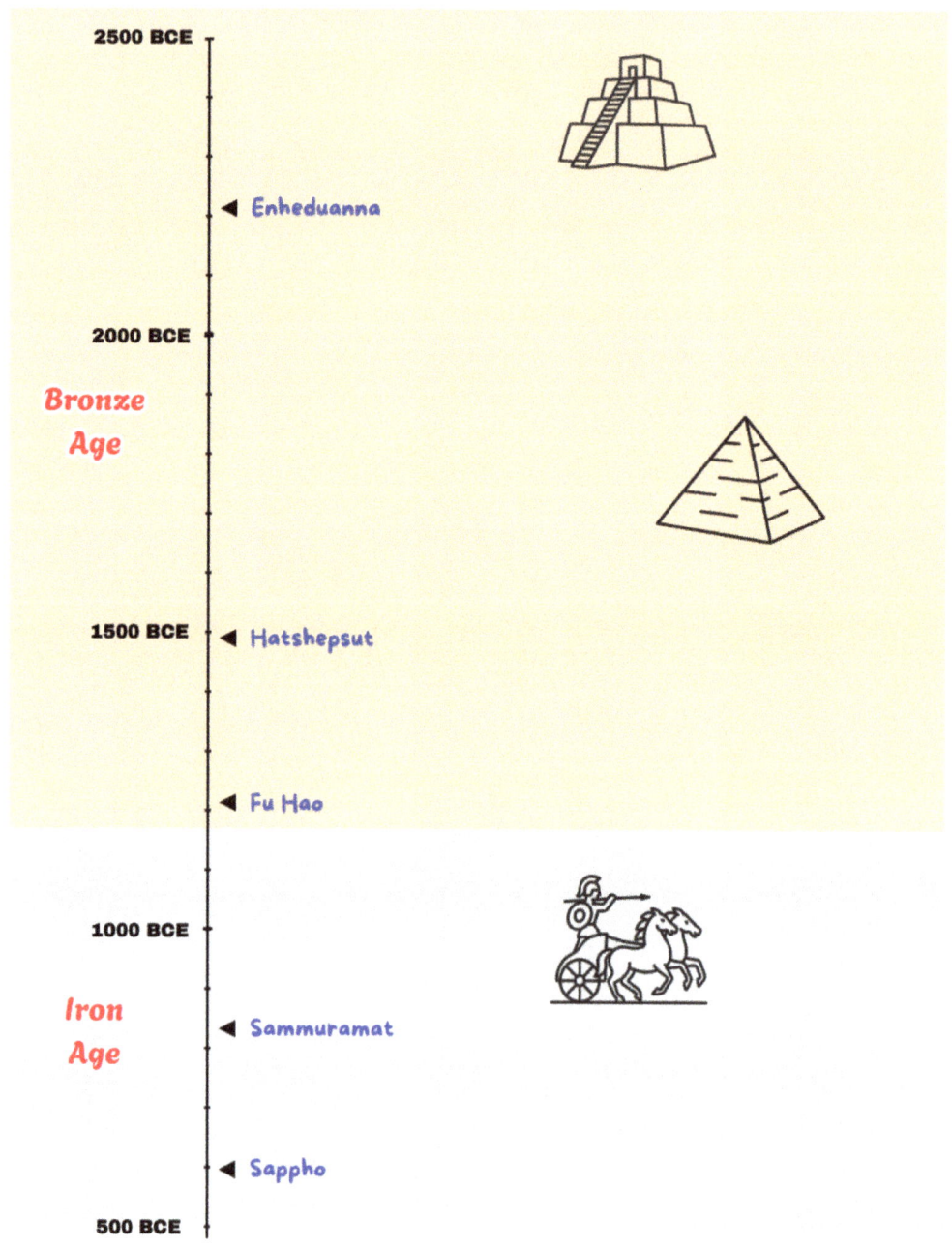

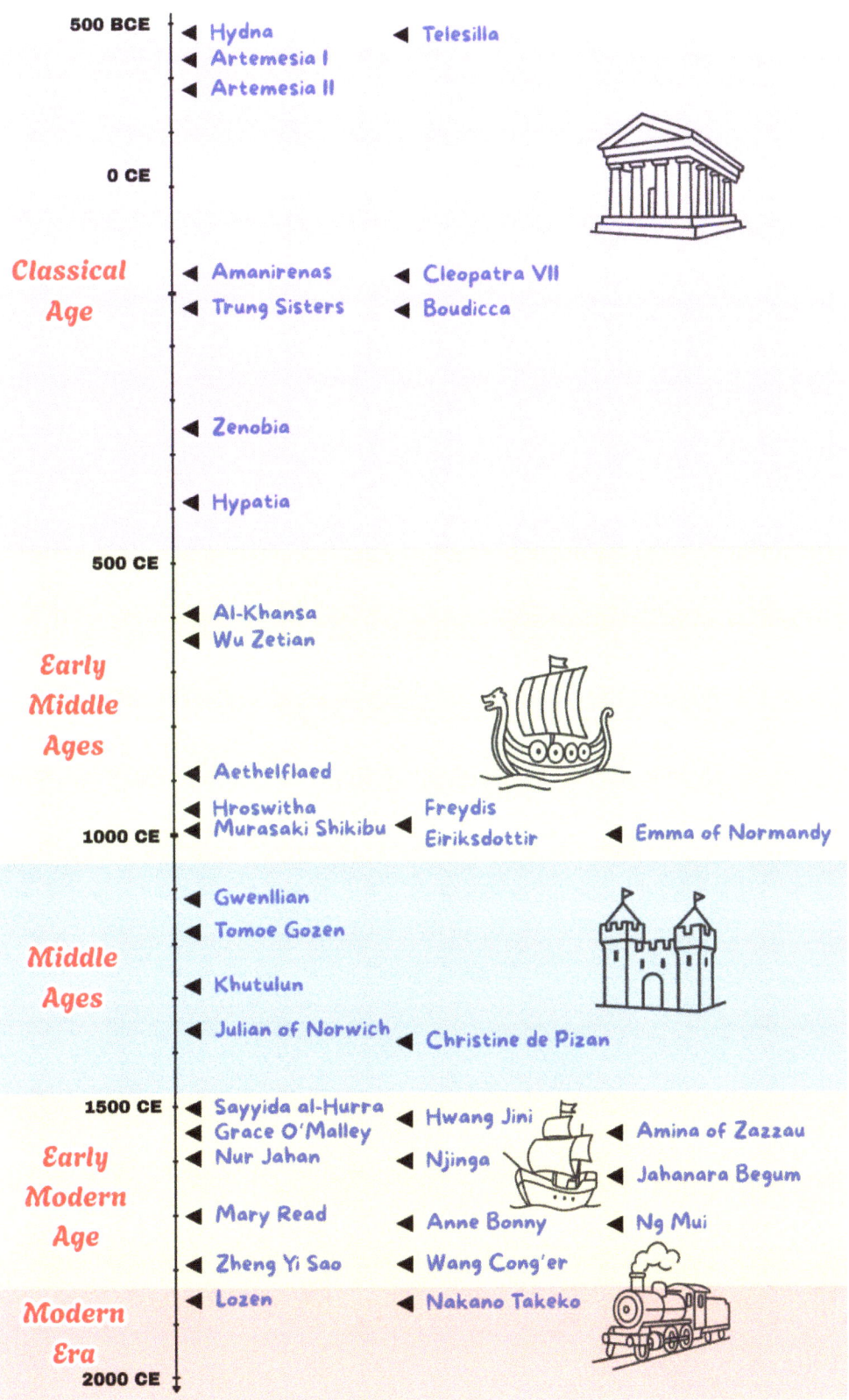

ENHEDUANNA
(En-hed-dwana)

Lived: Around 2,230 B.C.E.
Location: Sumeria (now Iraq)
Occupation: Priestess, Poet

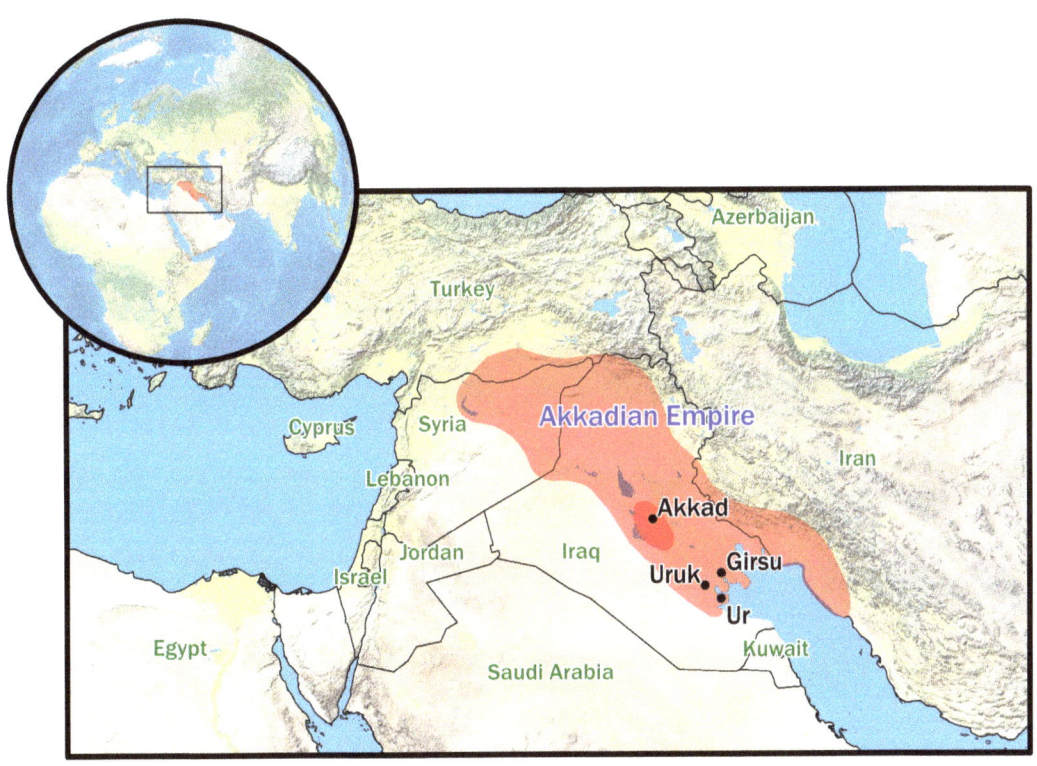

Enheduanna lived in Sumeria over 4,000 years ago. Her name is still known today because it appears on clay tablets with poems written on them.

e are starting right back in the earliest civilisation of the world. Enheduanna lived in one of the **very first empires** that existed, in ancient Sumeria. Today, this place is known as Iraq, in the Middle East.

Enheduanna was the daughter of *King Sargon*, who ruled over the *Akkadian Empire*. Cities had emerged long before this time, but Sargon brought these cities together under his rule and created the world's first empire.

> ### INTERESTING FACT:
> A 'civilisation' is a group of people who settled in one place and started to farm, rather than being nomadic hunter-gatherers. The earliest civilisation was Sumer, which existed from 5,500 B.C.E. Cities developed from about 4,000 B.C.E. as more people settled and began to build. Society became bigger. Sumer existed 3,000 years before the Akkadian Empire! King Sargon was the first person to unite cities through conquest in this way, becoming a single ruler of many places, and so creating an empire.

Enheduanna was a priestess. Priests and priestesses were very important and had a high status in their society, because they prayed to the gods and goddesses on behalf of people, to ask for good harvests and good fortune in their lives. The priests and priestesses performed important rituals in honour of the gods, and made sure people obeyed their rules.

There were many gods, and Enheduanna was a priestess of the moon god *Nanna*. Although she was important to Nanna, **Enheduanna wrote a lot of poems in praise of all the gods.** This was important, because people believed the gods needed to be pleased and praised, or they might bring bad luck to a place.

Enheduanna would have been very well respected by the people of all the cities and places that she visited, as they would **ask her to pray to the gods** for them. People would listen to what she said, believe her if she said they would have good or bad luck, and they would listen to any advice she gave them. As a priestess to the gods, Enheduanna would have been almost as important as her father, the king.

The poems of Enheduanna, written thousands of years ago, were only rediscovered in 1927! That is a *very* long time after Enheduanna lived. The reason that these poems lasted for thousands of years is because they were **written into clay tablets.** Paper did not exist back then. Clay tablets are much longer lasting than paper, and they were buried underground, which helped them to stay in good condition. It is because of these rediscovered tablets that Enheduanna is celebrated today as **the first person recorded in history as an author!**

Enheduanna's writings give us insight on a time and culture from our ancient past. They are important historically, archaeologically, and in a literary sense! Her poems were in praise of all the gods of the region, including the goddess Inanna – who was the goddess of love and war and the 'queen of heaven' – and also the moon god Nanna. One set of her texts, known as the Temple Hymns, is a collection of poems dedicated to each different god or goddess. Since the discovery of these clay tablets, the poems have been copied, to make sure they are preserved and not lost again.

This is what a **cuneiform tablet** looked like. The words were pressed into soft clay which hardened, preserving it for thousands of years.

This says: 'Enheduanna, priestess of the great moon god Nanna'

Sumerian writing was made up of a set of symbols known as *cuneiform*. This was a series of straight lines, quite different to any written language we have today. It took experts many years to unravel the mystery of cuneiform and to be able to translate it, copying it into modern languages including English.

We do not know if Enheduanna was the very first woman to be a priestess, or the first to write poetry. But **she is the first to be recorded** – that is, to have been discovered – and this is why she is so important today. Enheduanna's role shows us that women could and did hold such prominent positions of power, right back in the days of the very first civilisations.

Lines from a poem by Enheduanna, Priestess of Nanna, of the Akkadian Empire under King Sargon:

> *"Lady of all powers*
> *Lady of radiant Light,*
> *Beloved of Heaven and Earth*
> *Bejewelled crown..."*

INTERESTING FACTS:

The earliest ever story we know of is from this same area, Sumeria, and is called The Epic of Gilgamesh. It was written as a series of poems on clay tablets and is a tale of a hero king who performs mighty deeds. It was written in 2,100 B.C.E., and still exists as a published story today!

Writing began not for creative storytelling, but because it was needed for accountancy – looking after a business, trading goods, keeping records. These are the very first records of writing that we have.

Hatshepsut
(Hat–ship–soot)

Lived: 1507 B.C.E. - 1458 B.C.E.
Location: Egypt
Occupation: Pharaoh

Hatshepsut was the second female pharaoh (ruler) of Egypt, living more than 3,400 years ago. Ancient Egypt was a great civilisation with a very long history, dating back more than 5,000 years.

Hatshepsut ruled Egypt with her husband, *Thutmose II*. When he died, she ruled on behalf of his two-year-old son, *Thutmose III*. However, as he was so young, she took the mantle of power for herself and **became 'Pharaoh' – 'God-king'** – for about twenty years.

Although there had been one queen pharaoh before (that we know of for sure), Hatshepsut is better known from records that have survived. She had more power and she ruled for longer, in a time of peace and prosperity.

Hatshepsut dressed herself in male clothing and was depicted in statues and carvings as a male pharaoh. **This helped her to have and maintain the authority and respect that she needed to rule**, because the kingship was usually passed to male heirs, from father to son. Ancient Egypt had not had many female pharaohs, and by dressing herself this way, Hatshepsut was showing her advisers and her people that she was just as capable and worthy of ruling as any man.

Unlike the times of many of the women in this book, Hatshepsut's time was peaceful, and Egypt was doing well. Egypt thrived as a civilisation early on because the land was fertile and good for growing food, thanks to its long river, the Nile. Cities sprang up all along the river over the centuries.

Egypt is famous for its many pyramids, built over hundreds of years by its rulers – it also has lots of temples to its many different gods. **Hatshepsut ordered the construction of hundreds of such religious buildings,** which included many obelisks (large standing stones with inscriptions written on them). She also opened up trade routes, allowing more goods to come to and from Egypt. This helped to make the country rich. The tree resin frankincense was one of the items that came into Egypt, which Hatshepsut used to make kohl. She used this as eye makeup – the first known use of **kohl eyeliner!**

Hatshepsut must have been clever to have stayed as **pharaoh for twenty years**, which was an especially long time in those ancient days. But after her death, attempts were made to lessen her reputation: her image was removed from stone walls, statues removed and torn down, and her name taken off carvings. However, enough evidence still survived for us to discover her in modern times and to know her name and legacy. In a time and place that was dominated by male pharaohs, Hatshepsut carved out a place for herself, remaining firmly in control and improving her country through her buildings and trade routes.

Example of Hieroglyphs, it says 'Hatshepsut', the special shape is called a 'cartouche' and shows that it is the name of a <u>Pharaoh</u>

INTERESTING FACTS:

There were many dynasties of Egypt over its long history of civilisation. Each dynasty was ruled by people who were related (father handing the title on to son, for example), and a new dynasty was created when a different family took power, unrelated to the previous one. Hatshepsut was part of the Eighteenth Dynasty. This means that there were seventeen royal dynastic families before her time.

Sobekneferu, also known as Neferusobek, was the very first female pharaoh that we know of. 'Sobek' was the name of Egypt's crocodile god (Ancient Egypt had many gods, and many had the heads of animals). She ruled in the mid eighteenth century B.C.E. – about 300 years before Hatshepsut. She was also depicted in male clothing, and she ruled for just over three years. Not much is known about her, due to a lack of surviving objects and writings. Sobekneferu was part of the Twelfth Dynasty.

Fu Hao
(Foo How)

Lived: 1230 B.C.E. - around 1200 B.C.E.
Location: China
Occupation: Battle Queen

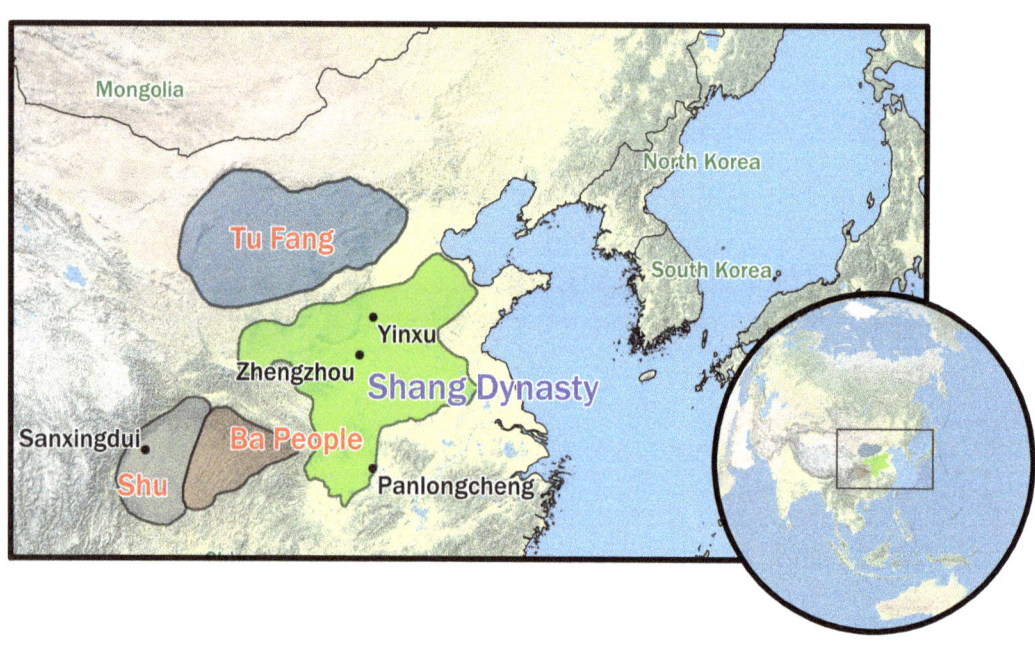

Fu Hao lived more than 3,000 years ago in the Shang Dynasty of China. She was one of sixty-four wives of the king, Wu Ding. (That's a lot of wives!) Fu Hao was foremost among them all.

It was a common custom for kings and other important men in ancient times, across many different cultures, to have a lot of wives. Having many wives showed how important a man was, and also ensured that he would have lots of children. Quite often, there would be a 'chief wife' – one who was the king's favourite and his equal (or almost equal). Fu Hao held this position, and **she was also a general** of King Wu Ding's armies.

China was not a unified country at this time but was split into different states, with kings and other leaders vying for control over territory. Fu Hao would have been highly trusted by the king to be a general in charge of the armies. She helped to expand her husband's territory by **leading military campaigns**. Although we do not know much about these very early days, there are written records stating that **at least 600 women** served in these armies.

Fu Hao, also known as Lady Hao, had her own land and her own wealth. **As a general, she led a force of 13,000 troops**. They won many battles, conquering nearby states and defeating many enemies. Fu Hao and Wu Ding were known as the *Shang Dynasty*, and they were at war with *Tu Fang*, a neighbouring state. With her 13,000 soldiers, Fu Hao defeated them in one decisive battle, using excellent military strategy, for which she was greatly respected.

After her death, **her husband continued to ask for her help by praying to her,** seeking good outcomes for his wars and political decisions. She was so loved and respected by her husband that he believed her spirit could help him.

Thousands of years later, in 1976, Fu Hao's tomb was discovered and opened. There were many items inside, including battle axes and other weapons – items not usually buried with women.

Fu Hao was clearly a powerful and active woman from so long ago in our history, but she was not the only one. One of Wu Ding's other wives, *Fu Jin*, was also a military leader, as well as looking after agriculture (farming and food). Most of our knowledge about them comes from archaeological finds, which include **inscriptions written on tortoise shells** about Fu Hao's military campaigns, and the requests from Wu Ding for her help.

INTERESTING FACT:

In Fu Hao's tomb, buried with her were:

More than 700 jade objects (jade was considered precious and incredibly special)

over 500 bone objects

over 400 bronze objects

And many weapons.

The amount and quality of burial objects shows how important a person was in their life. Fu Hao's tomb was one of great wealth and importance.

The top symbols say 'Fu Hao' in <u>Oracle Bone Script</u> - an ancient form of Chinese writing

The bottom symbols say 'Fu Hao' in a more <u>modern Chinese</u> script. Can you see how the modern symbols developed from the ancient ones?

SAMMURAMAT
(Sam-oo-ra-mat)

Lived: 850 B.C.E. - 798 B.C.E.
Location: Neo-Assyria
Occupation: Queen

Sammuramat was a queen who lived in Neo-Assyria, which covered Iraq, Iran, Turkey, Egypt, and Arabia. It was the largest empire of its time.

ammuramat originally ruled the *Neo-Assyrian Empire* with her husband. When he died, she continued to hold power for her young son, like so many female rulers did and would do after her. However, she is the **only queen of this empire to have stayed on the throne after the death of her husband**, and then to go on to rule by herself.

> ### INTERESTING FACT:
> The Neo-Assyrian empire lasted for over 300 years, from 911-609 B.C.E This empire was the first to use large cavalry forces, and they created new siege warfare tactics. They used relay stations to communicate over the vast distances of the empire, and their communication speed was not matched again in the middle east until the 19th century – that's about 1,000 years afterwards!

Sammuramat **led a military campaign** with her son (when he was grown up), and possibly even participated in the battle. We know this because there is a stone monument that records this fact. These stone monuments, which had writing or pictures inscribed on them, are known as *stele*, and they were used to record the great deeds of kings and to celebrate other great achievements. It was extraordinary for a woman to be recorded on a stele. **Sammuramat is the only female mentioned in a battle campaign** of the Neo-Assyrian Empire, but there are several other stelae that name Sammuramat, including one dedicated solely to her. She must have been powerful as a ruler and had great influence to have secured a stele just for her.

Interestingly, the title of 'queen' did not exist in the Neo-Assyrian language, as women were normally only the wife of the king. They were known instead as '*women of the palace*'. They were well regarded, as **they had their own wealth and oversaw their own staff of female administrators,** who looked after their estates and finances. Women of the palace were also in charge of religious affairs and performed important rituals to the gods.

Not much else is known of Sammuramat's life, as we only have the stele as a record of her lifetime. But we know that she was powerful and influential, and that she expanded the borders of her realm, making her empire larger. This would have gone down well with her advisers and the people of the kingdom.

Sammuramat is not mentioned in later Assyrian culture, probably because she was female, and they did not think her important enough to mention alongside the kings and rulers.

Over the next few hundred years, though, Sammuramat's name and reign survived, her story was told and retold, and **she was turned into a legend by the Ancient Greeks.** The name 'Sammuramat' became '*Semiramis*' in Greek, and a story was told of a woman who was born to a goddess, and who grew up to be a warrior, conquering many territories. Semiramis is a mythical figure, but one inspired by the great deeds of the Neo-Assyrian queen.

This is a <u>Lamassu</u>, a mythical creature; half human and half-winged bull!

The Assyrians used statues of Lamassu as fierce gate guardians to protect their palaces

INTERESTING FACTS:

Naqi'a – A Neo-Assyrian queen who lived around 728-669 B.C.E She did not hold power as a ruler herself, but as the wife of King Sennacherib (705-681 B.C.E), and then mother of the next king, Esarhaddon, she wielded a lot of influence, and is one of the most well known Neo-Assyrian queens. She is the only one to have issued a treaty. This treaty enforced loyalty of all of Assyria to her grandson, Ashubanipal, who ruled after his father. Naqi'a had a palace built for her son – highly unusual for a queen to order any constructions. She had her own estates in Babylon, which some documents hint that she may have ruled herself. She is only one of two queens to have been depicted in art.

Sappho
(Saffo)

Lived: 613 B.C.E. - 570 B.C.E.
Location: Lesbos, Greece
Occupation: Poet

Sappho lived in the time of Ancient Greece, when poetry and plays were regarded as high art forms, but women were not often counted among the great.

At this point in history, Greece had many busy and bustling cities, and its educated people enjoyed philosophy, art, mathematics, and poetry, as well as politics. Ancient Greece is famous for its large and beautiful white buildings, and for the many stories of its gods: *Zeus, Hera, Athena, Apollo*, to name a few.

But let us talk about Sappho: she lived on the Greek island of Lesbos. **Sappho was one of few women in this time who could read and write**. It was usually only educated, upper-class men who could read and who wrote poems, plays, and songs. Women were expected to be only wives and mothers. They were not allowed to be politicians or leaders, and they did not usually receive an education. But Sappho bucked these trends.

Sappho was **one of very few female poets** in this era. She wrote her own poems and they were so good that she was awarded the title of '*the Tenth Muse*'. This was a great honour indeed. The *Nine Muses* were minor deities in Greek culture, who reigned over all the arts including dance, song, and music. By giving Sappho this title, **she was elevated to the status of a 'master,'** and by some would be seen as almost god-like in her ability to craft beautiful poetry.

All we know of Sappho's early life is that she was born to a wealthy family, and that she had three brothers, two of whom are mentioned in her poems. She may also have had a daughter named Cleis, as there is a poem that Sappho wrote describing a beautiful daughter of hers by this name.

Sappho's poetry was meant to be **sung along to music**, and it was often about **love**. Much of her poetry is lost to us today, with only separate lines and fragments surviving. It is thought that she wrote around **10,000 lines of poetry**, and just 650 lines exist today. Only one of her poems still exists in full: *Ode to Aphrodite*. Aphrodite is the Greek goddess of love and beauty.

We know that the poems were recited among Sappho's female friends. Sappho may have even been their teacher, advising them on mastering the art of poetry. Her poetry was full of imagery and emotion, and **some of the phrases we use to describe love today** have come down to us from her writings.

Sappho was so well thought of, both during her own time and afterwards, that she was one of *the Nine Lyric Poets of Ancient Greece*. These were the most famous poets of the time, who were **considered worthy of study after their own lifetimes** –the best of the best. For a woman to be part of this group was an incredible (but very well deserved) feat. Sappho achieved such fame that she was even **depicted on vases and coins** in the centuries shortly after her own lifetime.

A line from Sappho's poetry, translated from her native Greek:

__Eros stirred my heart,__

__Like the wind stirring the trees__

(Eros was the god of love)

INTERESTING FACTS:

The Nine Muses were like the gods but had a lesser status. They were immortal, powerful beings. Each muse ruled over a particular art. They were:

Calliope – epic poetry

Clio (Kleio) – history

Polyhymnia – mime, also sacred poetry and hymns

Euterpe – music

Terpsichore – dance

Erato – lyric and love poetry

Melpomene – tragedy (as in sad songs, poems and plays)

Thalia – comedy (as in funny poems, songs and plays)

Urania – astronomy

TELESILLA
(Tell-e-sil-a)

Lived: 494 B.C.E. - unknown

Location: Argos, Greece

Occupation: Poet, Saviour of Argos

Telesilla was a poet who lived in the city of Argos in Greece. She was famous during her own lifetime for her poetry. She is also remembered for helping to save her city.

Telesilla, like Sappho before her, was a gifted poet. She became **one of the nine female lyric poets of Greece** – this was an alternative list of women only poets, who were so great that they were considered worthy of study by educated men of the time and after. She was so good, in fact, that **she had a form of poetry named after her:** the *Telesillan metre.*

Although very little of her poetry has survived to the present day, there are fragments of Telesilla's work that mention two of the Greek gods: *Apollo and Artemis.*

During Telesilla's time, there was war. The country 'Greece' did not exist then; instead, the land was split into **independent city-states** that often fought with each other. In 494 B.C.E., the army of Sparta marched to attack Argos, where Telesilla lived. Sparta was famous for its warriors, as its people believed that being a brilliant warrior was the greatest possible achievement. The men began training for war from the age of just seven, and joined the main army from age eighteen. No other Greek city-state could match Sparta for its warrior training.

Sparta marched to Argos, led by their king, *Cleomenes*. The fighting men of Argos marched out to meet the enemy some way from the city, and **were defeated on the field of battle** by the Spartans. This left their city defenceless, and the Spartans moved to take it.

When Telesilla saw the Spartan army approaching, she decided that **she was not going to let her city surrender without a fight!** She roused the city, gathering all the slaves, women, and old men (everyone who was left in the city), arming them with whatever weapons they could find. They climbed to the top of the city walls, where the invading enemy could see them. They stood brandishing their weapons and shouting down at the Spartans.

When the Spartan men saw that **women, slaves, and old men were defending the city**, this put them in a quandary: if they attacked and won, there would be no honour or glory in defeating slaves and women. If they lost, their shame would be great. Either way, they could not win. In the end, they took the only action they could: they withdrew from the city!

The celebrations were great in Argos, and in honour of this victory they gave the day the name of '*Hybristica*'. From then on, that day would be celebrated every year by having **women wear men's clothes and men wear women's clothes,** as a reminder that women had just as much courage as men did.

INTERESTING FACTS

Another famous female poet of this era was Anyte of Tegea, and she wrote short, beautiful poems for animals that had died. She wrote epitaphs for a horse, a bird, a locust, and a dolphin! Her work 'Epitaph to a Goat' reads: "The children, O billy-goat, have put purple reins on you and a muzzle on your bearded face, and they train you to race like a horse round the god's temple that he may look on their childish joy."

Sparta is also famous for the story of 'The 300'. In 480 B.C.E., Persia attacked Greece. In order to stop them and give all the Greek city-states time to get their armies together, a small force of 300 Spartans marched out to meet thousands and thousands of Persians. With a small band of allies from elsewhere, the Spartans held off the much mightier force of the Persians for three whole days! They were eventually defeated, but their brave sacrifice gave the rest of Greece time to prepare for attack.

Spartan warriors never backed down; it was considered shameful for them to do so. They would fight to the last man. In honour of this, there is an epitaph to those brave Spartan heroes, written on stone, and placed at the site of the battle, in Thermopylae:

> "Go tell the Spartan, stranger passing by,
>
> That here, according to our law, we lie."

HYDNA
(Hid-na)

Lived: 500 B.C.E. - unknown
Location: Scione, Greece
Occupation: Swimmer

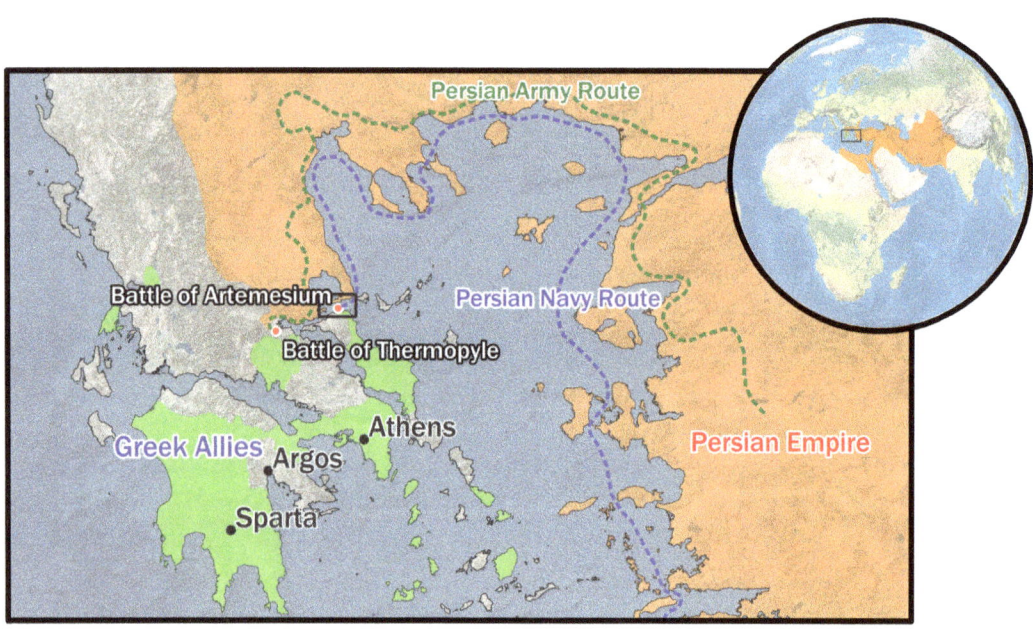

Hydna of Scione's story is brief, but she is remembered in history because of her courageous actions during the war between Greece and Persia.

The Persian king, *Xerxes*, had decided to invade Greece, as he wanted to make it part of his mighty empire. The *Persian Empire* was already huge, covering Turkey, Iran, Iraq, and almost reaching the border of India. But this was not enough for Xerxes; he wanted Greece as well. He engaged in a **naval battle with the Greeks in 480 B.C.E.**, and this fight became known as the *Battle of Artemisium*.

> ### INTERESTING FACT:
>
> The naval battle of Artemisium took place at the same time as the land battle at Thermopylae, where the Greek city-states of Athens, Sparta, Corinth and others stood against the Persian forces of Xerxes. The idea was that the Greek forces would block the Persian invasion both on land and by sea. The Greek side failed to hold the Persians on land, and when the Greek ships heard this news, they withdrew to Salamis, where another battle took place – now known as 'The Battle of Salamis,' which the Greek allies won, halting the Persian invasion.

Hydna's father, *Scyllias*, was a diving instructor, and he taught his daughter to swim. She was well known for her **strong swimming** and for being able to dive deep into the ocean.

Hydna was no soldier or hero, but an ordinary young woman. She and her father offered to help the Greek fleet as they were so good at swimming. They told the soldiers that they could swim over to where the Persian fleet were waiting, and then **sabotage** them. Of course, the Greek soldiers were delighted at this and agreed.

It was nighttime and dark when Hydna and Scyllias made their journey. The ocean would have been cold. And it was **ten miles to the Persian fleet**…. That is a *very* long way to swim! That distance would have taken about five hours to cover, and then they would have to swim back too. Hydna and her father must both have been confident in their abilities to brave such a long, dangerous journey.

When father and daughter reached the enemy Persian ships, they knew they would have to be careful and very quiet, so that the enemy soldiers did not see and capture them. With the great hulks of the large ships above them, Hydna and her father stayed in the water. They took the sharp knives they had carried with them and they **cut away the moorings** – the ropes that tied the ships in place, to keep them secure. This meant that **the ships were now loose and started moving, turning about and crashing into one another.** A few of them even sank. This meant there were fewer Persian ships for the Greek navy to have to fight when the battle began the next day.

This is all that we know of Hydna and her father. Nothing else is recorded about her life. However, we know that the Greeks were grateful to her and considered her actions important, because **they put up a statue to Hydna and her father.** This statue was placed at *Delphi*, which was a sacred place. It was a religious centre and the Oracle of Delphi was based here – she was a woman who spoke on behalf of the god *Apollo*. For a statue of Hydna to be put here was a great honour.

Although this is all that we know of Hydna, this one daring journey – a long, long swim to enemy ships, to cause damage and help their Greek army – was heroic enough to ensure her legacy.

HYDNA'S SWIM:

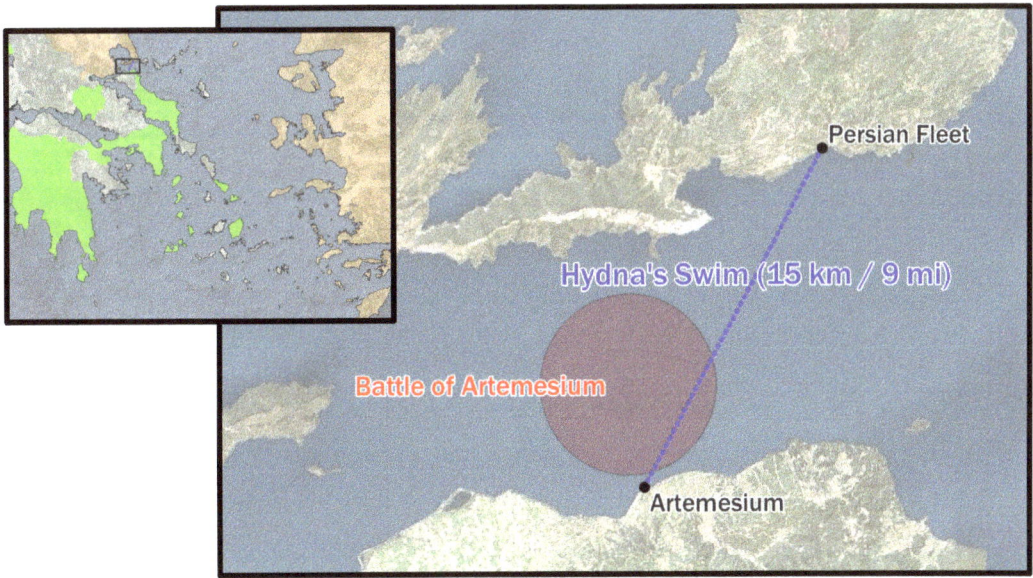

ARTEMISIA I
(Art-e-mis-ia the First)

Lived: 480 B.C.E - unknown
Location: Caria, Turkey
Occupation: Queen, Battle Commander

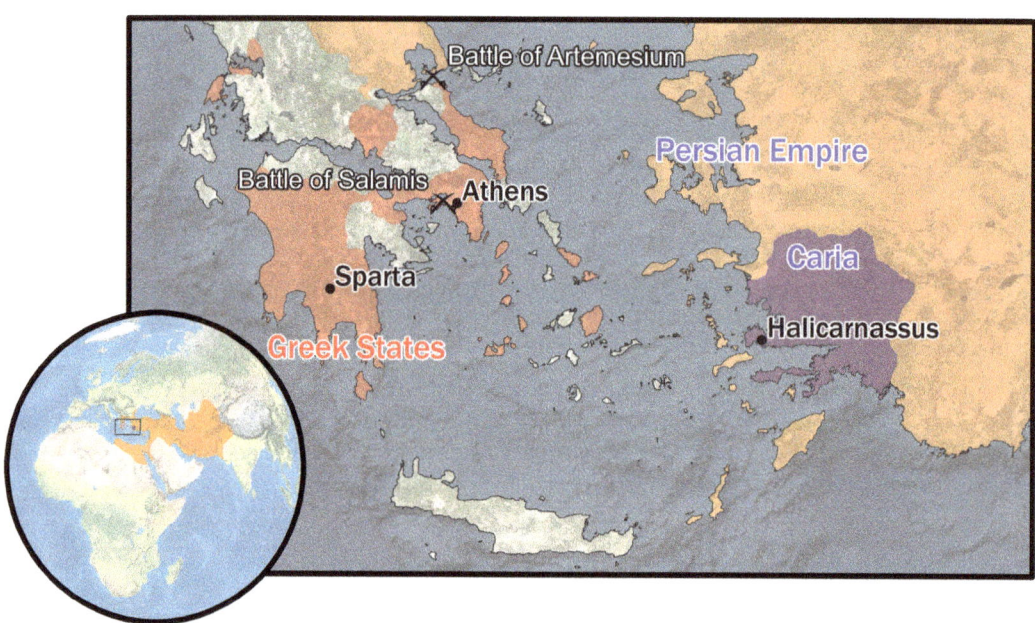

Artemisia I was a queen, ruling in her own right after the death of her husband. She was named after the Greek goddess Artemis, a moon goddess and hunter, who was usually depicted with a bow and was a patron of women.

Artemisia lived and ruled in an area of what is today Turkey. She was the queen of *Halicarnassus, the island of Kos, and also Nisyros and Kalymnos!* Although she was a queen, **Artemisia ruled a small area that came under the Persian Empire and the command of the great king Xerxes.** Persia was a large empire, covering today's Iraq, Iran, and Turkey. Artemisia was a lesser ruler under *Xerxes*, and if he called a war, all the kings and queens under him had no choice but to obey.

Xerxes was waging a war with Greece, which he wanted to make part of his empire. Artemisia had been involved in a battle in *Euboea* in Greece. Athens, the greatest Greek city-state, was evacuated to save all the people there. Athens was then burned to the ground by Xerxes and his forces, so after this, the Greeks were more determined to stop the Persians than ever.

After Euboea, Xerxes ordered everyone to attack the Greeks by sea, waging several naval battles. This is the same battle that Hydna of Scione took part in (see previous chapter), only with Artemisia on the opposite side to Hydna. **Artemisia owned five ships,** which she brought with her to fight the war. Although this does not sound like many, it was incredibly unusual for a woman to own a single ship, let alone a fleet of them.

At *The Battle of Salamis,* which was the second naval battle of the war, Artemisia did not think the Persians could win – in fact, **she was the only one of all Xerxes' commanders to advise him against the battle**, as she believed that the enemy was stronger than them and could overpower the Persian fleet. Xerxes was impressed with Artemisia speaking her mind and giving her counsel, but he decided to go ahead and engage in battle anyway. **Artemisia stayed on board** one of her ships, commanding from the deck during the naval fight. She was well known by her enemies, the Greeks, and **a bounty of 10,000 drachmae was put on her head** by leaders in Athens, who found it "intolerable" that a mere woman should be a fleet commander!

During the sea battle, Xerxes and his advisers watched from land. At one point, Artemisia's ship was being chased by the enemy, and as she sailed away from them, she found herself blocked by ships belonging to her own side. The forces were fighting in a narrow straight (not in the wide-open sea), so they only had a little room to manoeuvre. The Persian ships were in her way, so to get out of this situation, **Artemisia ordered her men to take down their colours (the sail) and ram them – ships that were on their own side!** As they rammed their way through, the Persian ships broke with the force and the men went spilling overboard. The Greek ship, seeing this, then assumed they had been chasing one of their own (they hadn't!) and turned away!

Xerxes was told by his adviser that Artemisia had sunk a Greek ship. Because they were so far away from the battle, **no one could see what really happened and everyone assumed (of course!) that Artemisia had destroyed the enemy.** She got away with it, too, because none of the men from the rammed ships survived.

Xerxes' side eventually lost the battle, but he valued Artemisia and her contribution to the fight so much that **he gave her a full suit of armour** as a gift! He also asked for her advice once again on what he should do next. Xerxes saw two options: either lead his troops to battle on mainland Greece, or withdraw, leaving one of his generals in charge. Artemisia advised him to leave his general, Mardonius, in Greece, and for Xerxes himself to return home. She told him that if Mardonius won against the Greeks, then the glory would belong to Xerxes as the great king. However, if Mardonius were to lose, then the failure would belong to him alone. This time, **Xerxes listened to Artemisia** and left Mardonius in Greece while he went back home.

Artemisia was ordered to go to Ephesus with Xerxes' sons, and this is the last we know of this courageous, fleet commanding queen. Although this story shows that Artemisia was ruthless, she must have been incredibly brave, clever, and cunning to take part in wars and sail out with her ships into a fierce battle.

INTERESTING FACT:

Another notable Greek woman who took part in a battle was Cynane (approx. 357-323 B.C.E). She was the daughter of Philip the Second of Macedon, and half-sister to Alexander the Great. Cynane joined her father on a campaign in 344 B.C.E, where she met and faced the Illyrian queen, Caeria, who was on the opposing side. They fought in hand-to-hand combat, and Cynane won. Cynane was trained in warfare by her mother, and she continued the tradition by training her own daughter, Eurydice.

ARTEMISIA II
(Art-e-mis-ia the Second)

Lived: 395 B.C.E. - 351 B.C.E.
Location: Caria, Turkey
Occupation: Queen, Battle Commander

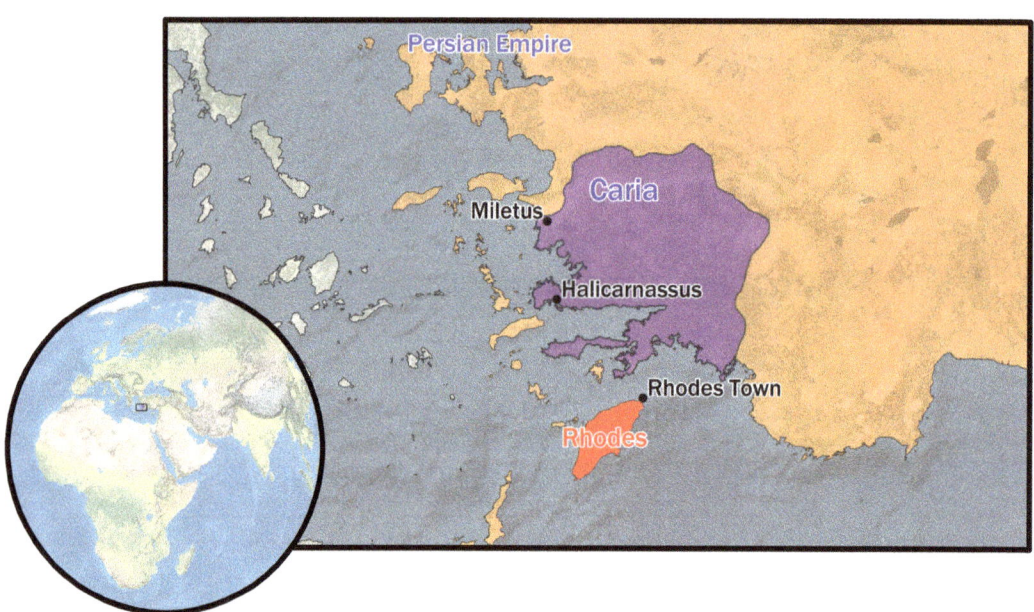

There was a second Artemisia of Caria, who was also queen. She came about 100 years or so after Artemisia I, and like her namesake, was also a strategist and commander.

Artemisia II ruled with her husband, *Mausolus*, until his death in 353 B.C.E. She was so upset when he died that she built the *Mausoleum at Halicarnassus*, which became **one of the seven wonders of the world!** It is from the name 'Mausolus' that the word *'mausoleum'* comes from.

> ### INTERESTING FACT:
>
> A 'mausoleum' is a small building in which we can place those who have died. It's like a little house. Many years after Mausolus and Artemisia lived, nobility would build mausoleums to house their family members after they died.

The island of Rhodes – a country near to Caria – decided to invade, as they **objected to a woman being a ruler.** Ruling was the realm of men, after all! The king of Rhodes probably saw this as a good opportunity to take more land for himself and increase his own status and power.

However, Artemisia heard about this and decided she was not going to meekly give up her country to those upstart Rhodians! She came up with a plan. When the men of Rhodes were sighted on their way across the sea, **Artemisia ordered some of her men to hide in boats** in a secret harbour. She also ordered more soldiers to hide in her city, setting up an ambush. With all her people quietly hidden, they waited for the enemy to arrive.

When the Rhodians came, they moored their ships at the main harbour, not realising there was a hidden harbour nearby full of enemy soldiers. They marched inland to take the city, completely unaware that they had been seen. This, of course, left their ships unmanned and empty... Seeing the soldiers marching off towards her city, **Artemisia then sailed her fleet out from the hidden harbour** to the enemy ships, which she and her men then boarded.

Meanwhile, the men of Rhodes entered the city, shouting and waving their weapons. But they were confused to find it quiet, with no one walking about. Suddenly, **Artemisia's soldiers leapt out from their hiding places,** taking the enemy by surprise – and so the Rhodians were easily captured and defeated.

At the same time, Artemisia and her men sailed towards Rhodes. The locals saw the ships coming and recognised them, thinking that their own soldiers were returning. They stood on the docks, cheering and waving. **Imagine their** surprise, then, when the ships pulled up to the harbour, and out jumped Artemisia and her soldiers! They captured Rhodes easily, and so the poor king of Rhodes – who had expected to capture Caria and remove Artemisia without struggle – found himself with his own island taken from him instead.

Like her namesake, this Artemisia also seems to have been ruthless, cunning, and clever. Maybe there is something powerful about being named after *Artemis* – the goddess of the hunt and the bow!

This is what we think the **Mausoleum of Mausolus** may have looked like. Very large and very grand!

Cleopatra VII
(Clee-o-patra the Seventh)

Lived: 70 B.C.E. - 30 B.C.E.
Location: Egypt
Occupation: Pharaoh

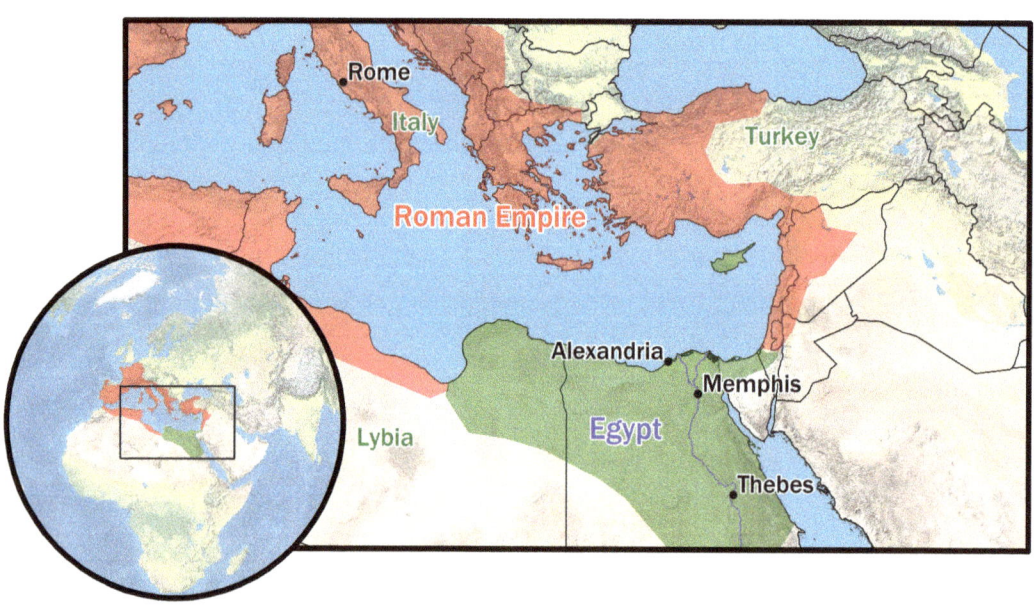

Cleopatra VII is the most famous of the Egyptian female pharaohs, and one of the most famous Egyptian rulers altogether. Extremely clever and politically smart, she was the seventh of her name – 'Cleopatra' was a popular name for royal girls!

Cleopatra lived and ruled at the same time as *Julius Caesar*, the famous ruler of the *Roman Empire*. By this time, Egypt was already ancient, and Rome, much newer than Egypt, was at its height. They were the biggest powers in the ancient world, so **Cleopatra knew that she had to be politically clever** to negotiate and deal with Rome.

Cleopatra co-ruled with her brother, who was also her husband (!!!). This was considered normal for Egyptian rulers, as **they believed that the pharaohs were the human forms of their chief gods,** *Osiris* and *Isis*. Sisters and brothers married to keep the royal bloodline pure, with the queen being the embodiment of Isis and the king the embodiment of Osiris.

The pharaohs at this time were of Greek descent, known as the *Ptolemy Dynasty*. The first Greek ruler of Egypt, *Ptolemy*, was in 305 B.C.E. (300 years before Cleopatra lived). So Cleopatra came from a Greek family, and they had always spoken Greek – but, as they lived and ruled in Egypt, their culture and beliefs were different from those who lived in Greece. **Cleopatra loved learning, and she spoke multiple languages**, being the first royal of her line to learn and speak Egyptian. She was well versed in politics and enjoyed studying at the great library of Alexandria.

Cleopatra's brother was still quite young when they married and took the throne of Egypt. He had an adviser, who told the young pharaoh, also named Ptolemy, what he should think and do. Cleopatra disagreed with this adviser and so they often argued. In time, this conflict turned into a **civil war,** with people in Egypt taking sides between the two rulers. There was fighting and rioting, and **Cleopatra was forced to flee Egypt** for a time.

Caesar of Rome also had a civil war on his hands, fighting *Pompey*, his Roman rival, for control. Pompey visited Egypt to ask for help against Caesar and was killed by Ptolemy, who thought this would make Caesar happy. When Caesar came to Egypt, he was angered by the killing of Pompey who, although his enemy, was also an important Roman. Caesar remained in Egypt for a time, trying to help calm the fighting.

Cleopatra made her way back to Egypt, **smuggling herself secretly into the palace** and into Caesar's room. She persuaded him to become her ally. With Caesar's help, she retook her throne next to her brother. But there were still arguments and disagreements. Soon, another riot followed, and **this time Cleopatra's side won**. Ptolemy fled by ship, but drowned at sea. From here on, **Cleopatra was the undisputed pharaoh of Egypt.** She and Caesar fell in love and were the two most powerful rulers of their time.

Soon after, with Caesar having returned to Rome, Cleopatra had a son. She named her son *Caesarion* ('Little Caesar'), and she sailed to Rome with him to introduce him to Caesar, who was his father. Cleopatra wanted her child declared publicly as Caesar's son, because this would make him the heir to the empires of both Egypt and Rome. But Caesar refused to do this for political reasons.

Nevertheless, Cleopatra stayed in Rome, spending time with Caesar. The Roman nobles were aghast at Cleopatra's presence and demeanour – **here was a female ruler in their midst, bowing to no-one, talking and eating with men, speaking to Caesar like a friend!** This was not how Roman women behaved, and many found it strange and distasteful. But Caesar seemed to love Cleopatra, and while she was in Rome, he asked for her advice on building projects. Designs for buildings were upgraded on her suggestions.

> ### INTERESTING FACT:
> **Cleopatra was still in Rome when Caesar was assassinated by the senate (the Roman council). They had had enough of his controlling ways and his greed for total power. One fateful day, Caesar was betrayed by his friends and his life ended. Cleopatra knew this was a dangerous time for her, as the Romans did not like her. A riot broke out when the death of Caesar became known, but Cleopatra managed to escape and went back to Egypt.**

When civil war broke out again in Rome, **Cleopatra decided to ally** with the Roman *Mark Antony*. They too fell in love, and Cleopatra had three more children with him. Mark Antony asked for some of her Egyptian forces to help fight his war – Cleopatra agreed, but only if Mark Antony gave her back some territory owned by Rome which had once belonged to Egypt. He agreed, and **Egypt had the most territory that it had ever had** thanks to Cleopatra's efforts.

The war in Rome went on for a number of years, with factions fighting over who would become the next Caesar. Mark Antony's enemies were horrified that he had given away territory to Cleopatra, and so they also **declared war on Egypt**. Eventually, Mark Antony was overwhelmed. His enemies invaded

Egypt and got into the capital. Knowing that the Romans would not treat her kindly, Cleopatra chose to end her own life instead of being captured. She managed to get a message to Mark Antony, who came to be with her and die by her side.

Cleopatra was the **last pharaoh of Egypt.** After her, Rome ruled in Egypt, ending the dynasty of pharaohs that had been going for thousands of years. Despite wars with her brother and in Rome, Cleopatra managed to create some stability in her country, improving trade and overseeing important temple buildings. The people loved her because she spoke Egyptian and tried to make life better for them, especially farmers. She gave wealth to places of education and the arts.

Her involvement with Rome – including her relationships with two of its most important men – as well as her knowledge, cleverness, and skill in governance all created a lasting legacy for this last and most famous female pharaoh.

INTERESTING FACTS:

The Ancient Egyptians had many gods, and a lot of them had the heads of animals. Osiris was the king of the gods, and Isis was the queen. There was also Anubis, Ra, Horus, and Hathor, to name just a few.

Cleopatra's daughter, Cleopatra Selene, later married the king of Numidia in north Africa and ruled that kingdom with him. To her new country, she brought scholars and artists who had been at her mother's court, to create a centre of learning and culture.

Cleopatra is one of the most iconic women who ever lived, with many films, shows and books about her. However, we don't actually know what she looked like. Her tomb was never found, and there are no statues of her.

Amanirenas
(A-marny-ray-nus)

Lived: 57 B.C.E. - 10 B.C.E.
Location: Sudan
Occupation: Queen

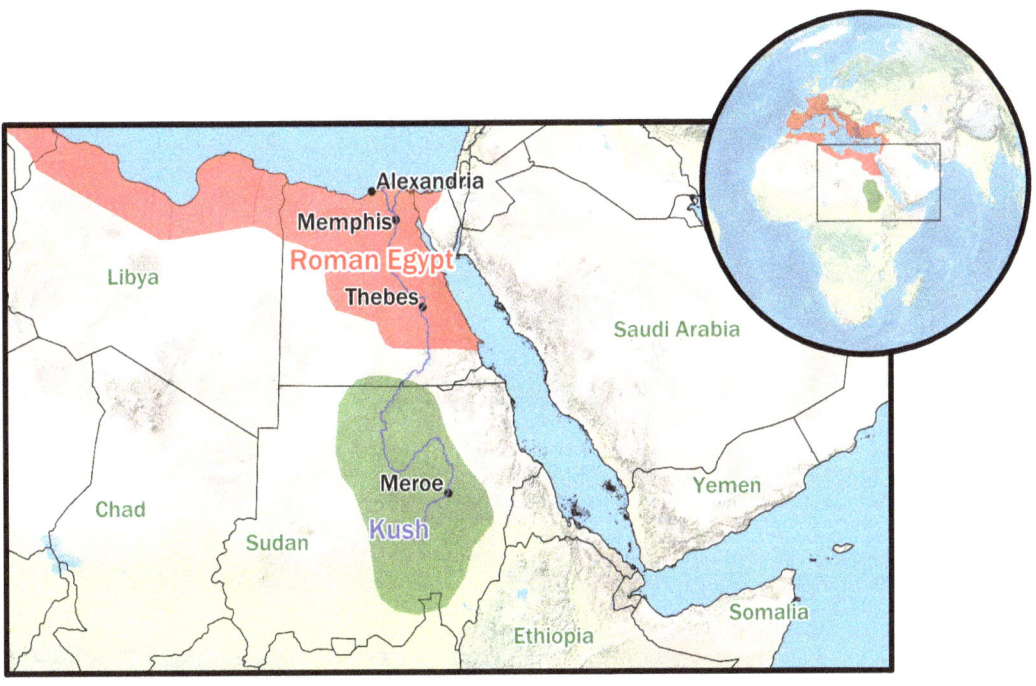

Queen Amanirenas ruled just over 2,000 years ago in the Kingdom of Kush, which is today Sudan in Africa. Her reign lasted for about thirty years, from 40 B.C.E. until her death in around 10 B.C.E.

Amanirenas was a *Kandake* – a female ruler. The Kushite kingdom had several queen rulers and Amanirenas is the most famous of them all because **she fought against the Roman Empire.** Rome was a large military power, and their empire spanned most of Europe and parts of North Africa.

Amanirenas' kingdom was just south of Egypt, and for the first few years of her reign, she ruled at the same time as Cleopatra VII - they may even have been friends as they were so close to each other. But the Romans took Egypt in about 30 B.C.E., and this made the queen of the Kush nervous, as Rome liked to expand and take territory. With Rome on her border, the queen was not going to bow down and let them take her country! Instead, she decided to fight. **Amanirenas commanded thousands of soldiers** and together they were determined to resist the Romans, stopping them from entering their kingdom.

The Kushite forces struck at the Romans, with **the queen fighting alongside her men.** She was a **fierce warrior** and her army kept the Roman forces in check, blocking them from making any advances. Instead, the opposite happened – Amanirenas and her soldiers managed to advance themselves and **took several Roman cities!** The queen knocked down any statues of the Roman emperor that she came across, just to show how much she disliked Rome. She even buried the head of one statue in her capital, Meroe, so that it was stamped on by people's feet! Her forces managed what many could not: **to halt the oncoming threat** of the Roman army.

The war, which has become known as the *Meroitic War*, went on for about **five years,** and in that time, Rome could not gain what they wanted. They made no advances and were continually losing men to Amanirenas' forces. Eventually, the queen negotiated a peace treaty. This treaty was so successful that **peace between the empire and the Kushite kingdom lasted for over 200 years!** This peace treaty, an agreement with Rome, was a huge victory for Amanirenas, given that Rome was a large military force that was used to winning its battles and expanding its empire.

Amanirenas had halted the expansion of Rome. It is for this reason that the Kushite queen has kept her well-deserved place in history.

INTERESTING FACTS:

Here's a list of all the known Kushite Kandakes (female rulers). Dates and order of Kandakes are approximate and the 'best guesses' of experts.

Nahirqo – c.145 B.C.E. Earliest known Kandake.

Amanirenas – c.57 B.C.E. Fought Rome.

Amanishakheto – Late B.C.E / Early first century C.E. Successor to Amanirenas. Known for many building projects.

Shanakdakhete – Early first century C.E. Known to have built a temple.

Nawidemak – Early first century. A picture on her tomb shows her wearing clothes usually worn by men.

Amanitore – Ruled jointly with her son in the middle of the first century C.E., during a prosperous time. Known for restoring several temples and constructing new buildings.

Amanikhatashan – First or second century C.E. Only known from an inscription on her tomb; no further information about her reign.

Amanikhalika – Probably second half of second century C.E. Known from an inscription on a tomb.

The Trung Sisters

Lived: 14 C.E. - 43 C.E.
Location: Vietnam
Occupation: Rebel Leaders

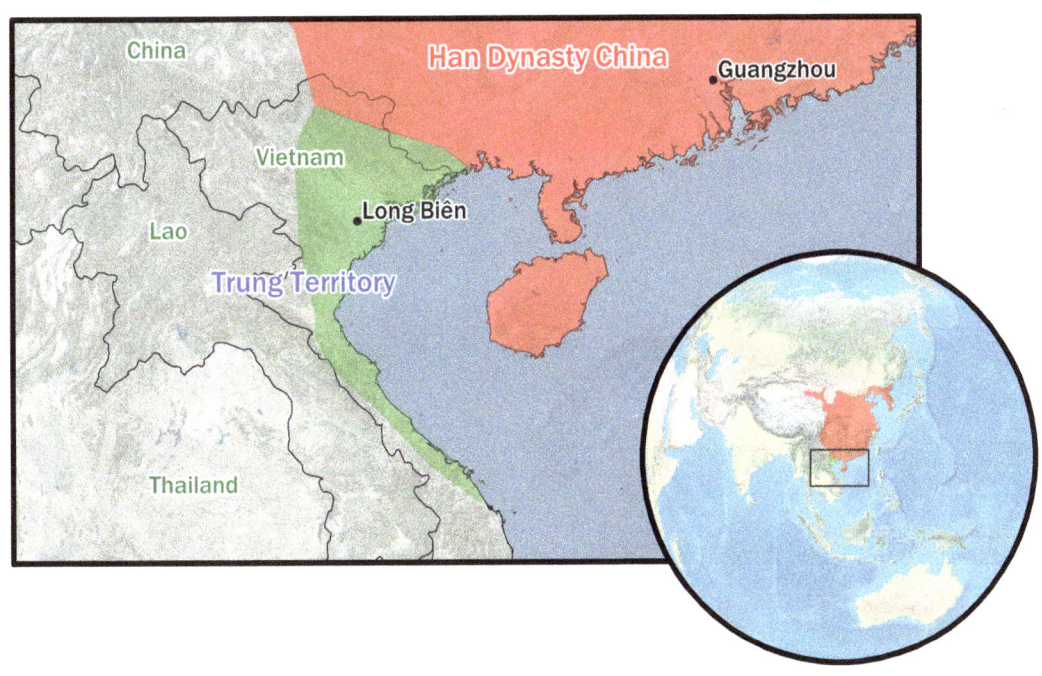

Trung Trac and Trung Nhi are known for leading a rebellion against Chinese occupation in Vietnam about 2,000 years ago.

Trung was the family name of these sisters, which is given first in some cultures, such as Vietnamese. The father of the Trung sisters was a local lord, so the family were very wealthy and had a high status.

However, at this time, Vietnam was ruled by China, and many of the local people were unhappy about this. Before, women in Vietnam could inherit land and property, but they were not allowed to do so under Chinese rule. Thanks to their father, **both the Trung sisters were highly educated,** particularly in literature and martial arts.

Trung Trac was the eldest sister, and she married a local lord, *Thi Sach*. Together they **plotted a rebellion** against the Chinese rulers. However, the plot was discovered and Thi Sach was taken away and killed by the Chinese governor. This enraged Trung Trac, and she was determined to avenge her husband.

Trung Trac and her sister Trung Nhi roused their people to rebel against the Chinese in the year 40 C.E. The sisters must have had influence, because they managed to **gather an army and lead it as generals.** The army marched to free their people from Chinese rule. Despite being common folk with no training in warfare, the Trung sisters' army took **sixty-five settlements** within a single year, also gaining the support of the people in each place. Their army included many women, around thirty-six of whom also became generals – including the Trung sisters' mother.

Due to this success, **the sisters were able to create their own new nation,** which stretched between Vietnam and Southern China. This new state, independent from China, brought back the **rights and freedoms for women** that they had known before Chinese rule. Both sisters ruled together, although Trung Trac was formally named as queen.

From their new nation, the sisters planned further assaults on their enemy. Although their army was smaller and not as well trained or armed as the Chinese military, they still succeeded in winning battles, partly because the Chinese government was slow to react to the rebellion.

The Trung sisters **ruled for about three years**, fighting their enemies and looking after their people. Eventually though, their army was defeated, as they were unable to hold out against the bigger, mightier Chinese army who finally became organised and pushed back. The rebellion came to an end in 43 C.E.

The legend of the sisters has rippled down through the years, **inspiring stories and poems,** and even further rebellions. Temples and shrines were erected to the sisters as a reminder of their courage and fearless bravery.

INTERESTING FACTS:

China ruled Vietnam from 111 B.C.E., which was just over 100 years before the Trung sisters lived. They continued to rule until 938 C.E. – that's another 900 years after the Trung sisters. There were many rebellions in Vietnam throughout this time.

The Trung sisters are often depicted riding elephants into battle!

The sisters are still seen as heroines in Vietnam today, and there is a national holiday in their honour. There are also many statues of the Trung Sisters still standing.

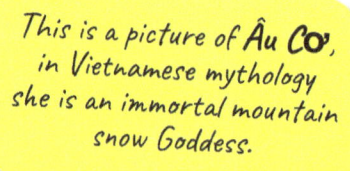

This is a picture of **Âu Cơ**, in Vietnamese mythology she is an immortal mountain snow Goddess.

She married the an ancient King, the **Dragon Lord of Lac** and is believed to be the mother of Vietnamese culture

BOUDICCA
(Boo-dee-ka)

Lived: Around 25 C.E. - 61 C.E.
Location: East Anglia, England
Occupation: Warrior Queen

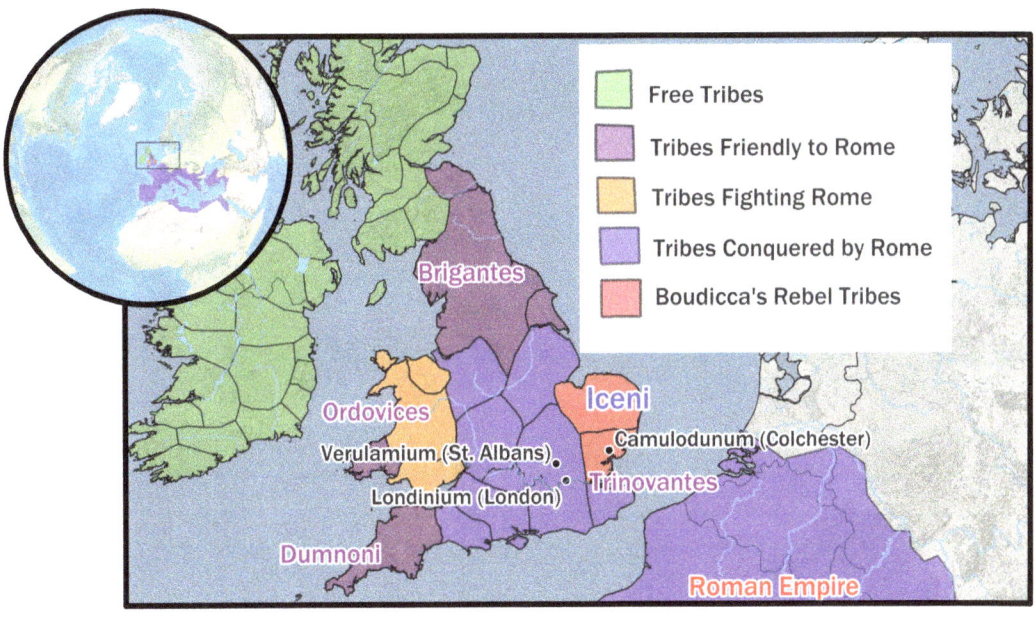

Boudicca was a Celt, who were the native people of Britain. She was part of a tribe known as the Iceni, who lived in Norfolk, England. England was split into lots of kingdoms with many Celtic tribes, and each had their own king or chieftain. Boudicca led a revolt against the Romans.

In 43 C.E., the new emperor of Rome, *Claudius*, sent some of his army to conquer Britain. With its large empire spread all across Europe, **Rome had been trading with Britain** for some time and now wanted to make it part of its empire, too. So Boudicca grew up seeing her country invaded and conquered, with Roman armies settling and taking charge.

The Celtic people lived a very different way of life to the Romans, so some of the tribes were not happy about this Roman takeover. But **each of the Celtic tribes had their own chieftain and customs,** so overall there was an uneasy peace between the Romans and the Celts across the country. Some tribes traded happily with the Romans, while others were grumbling quietly about rebellion. The Romans did not treat the native peoples well, frequently taking their land, crops and property for their own. Because of this, Rome kept armies in Britain to prevent any rebellions.

Boudicca was a **queen of the Iceni tribe** in what is now Norfolk. She was married to the chieftain *Prasutagus*. When he died, Boudicca expected her daughters to inherit half of his property, with the other half going to the Romans as was the custom. The Celts treated men and women equally, with **women able to own and inherit property and wealth.** However, the Romans refused to recognise that women could own any property, as women in Rome could not. They took all of Prasutagus' property, along with the rulership of the Iceni tribe.

Boudicca was absolutely furious. She challenged the Romans, wanting her property back. In return for this, she and her two daughters were treated very badly by the Romans, humiliated by them and publicly flogged. It was this terrible treatment that sparked **Boudicca's rebellion** – finally having had enough of the Romans taking everything that they fancied, Boudicca inspired her tribe to rebel.

She became the Iceni leader and **gathered her tribe ready for war.** The call went out, word spread, and other tribes who had had enough of the Romans came to join them.

The Roman army, which was large and organised, were at first taken by surprise. They were used to winning everywhere they went, although there were rebellions here and there – but **Boudicca led the tribes to victory** against the Roman town of *Camulodunum* (now called Colchester). The city was their capital and many Romans lived there; the Celtic army sacked the city and set it on fire. They then moved on toward *Londinum* (London) and *Verulamium* (St. Albans), which they also destroyed. The Celts then wiped out a detachment of the Ninth Legion made up of several thousand men, which was a massive victory.

> ### INTERESTING FACT:
>
> 'Boudicca' was not this heroine's real name. We don't know what her real name was, but 'Boudicca' means 'victory' or 'victorious'. It was a title given to her for her successful strategy against the Romans.
>
> Boudicca is known to us as a woman with flame red hair and riding a war chariot led by horses.
>
> The Celts loved their horses and valued them as beings of great wealth.

The Roman leaders did not, at first, believe their soldiers' **tales of a woman not only fighting, but appearing to lead** in the fights. In Roman custom, a woman in warfare was unthinkable! Regardless, Roman leaders soon became concerned with the victories of the Celts and knew that they had to do something to halt them. In the many skirmishes and battles that followed, thousands of people were killed on both sides.

Eventually, under a new British Roman governor, *Suetonius Paulinus*, the Roman army gathered and marched to a decisive battle. The might of the Celts was impressive – they outnumbered the Romans by thousands. But **Romans fought as organised units**, following directions under their captains, whereas the Celts fought as individuals. That battle, known as *the Battle of Watling Street,* was to be the absolute victory for the Romans, quashing the Celtic rebellion utterly.

No one knows what happened to Boudicca after this; there is no surviving record of how she died. Some say she was killed by the Romans. Some say that she took poison rather than risk being captured. Her body was never found (as far as we know), and so she may even have escaped, possibly fleeing to another country.

Boudicca's courage and fearlessness in the face of such a mighty empire, and her victories against Roman towns and cities, have ensured her place in history.

INTERESTING FACT:

Celts were very religious and their religious leaders, known as druids, were law makers, story tellers, historians, and made prayers to the gods. The Romans attacked the home of the druids in Ynys Mon (Anglesey), North Wales, in 60 C.E. This attack may have been another reason for Boudicca's rebellion. Roman forces had to leave Ynys Mon to deal with the new threat from Boudicca.

The attack on the druids had a significant impact on the Celtic way of life, destroying the people who kept their laws and history. After this, the Romans were fully in control in Britain until they left in around 409 C.E. Throughout this time there were many rebellions across England, Wales and Scotland.

Boudicca releasing a **hare** before battle, to bring her army **luck**. Hares, as well as many other animals were **sacred** to the Celts

Zenobia
(Ze-no-bia)

Lived: 240 C.E. - 274 C.E.
Location: Palmyrene Empire, Syria
Occupation: Queen

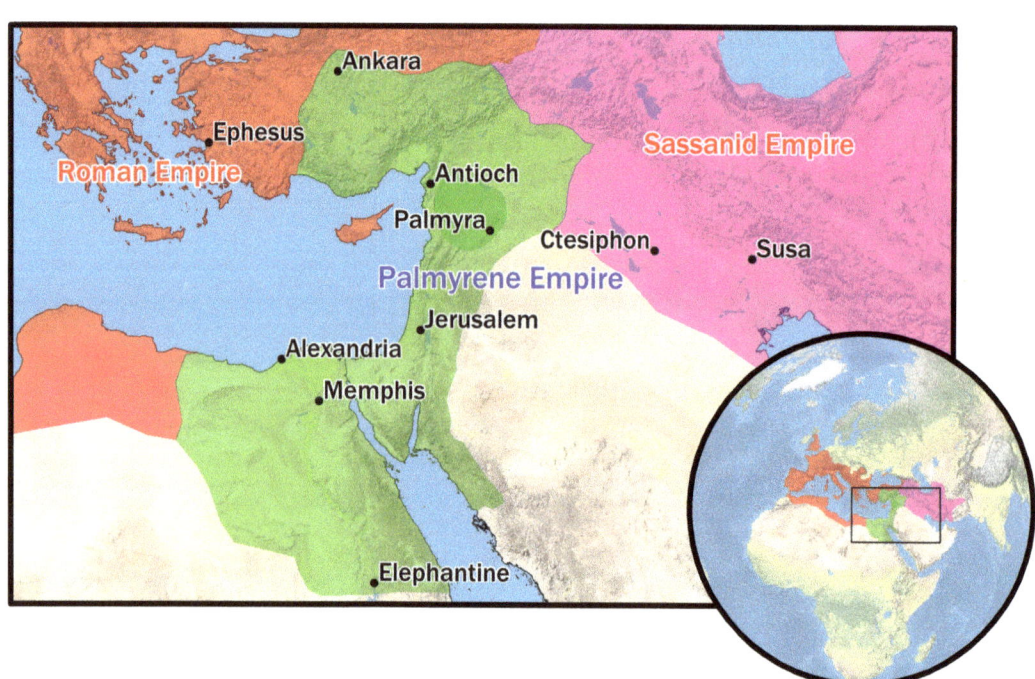

Zenobia was a queen who reigned in a region of Syria, at the time of the Roman Empire. She fought to free her country from Roman rule.

Zenobia was a noblewoman in Syria. She is also known as Bat-Zabbai and Al-Zabba. She married *Odaenathus*, who was the chief (or lord) of *Palmyra*, Syria. He was an ally of Rome, and **his territory was part of their greater empire**. Odaenathus fought against their enemies, pushing back the Persians who were trying to invade, and as thanks for his successes Rome made him king of the region. Zenobia herself had a noble heritage, **claiming that she was descended from the Greek rulers of Egypt**, *Ptolemy* and *Cleopatra*.

In 267 C.E., Odaenathus and his son were riding back from a battle when they were both ambushed and killed. Zenobia became the queen regent, holding onto power until her younger son, *Vaballathus*, became old enough to rule.

Palmyra was important to Rome, because of its location. It was well positioned to hold back their enemies, but it was also important for trade – it lay on the famous *silk road*, so lots of goods and merchants came through, creating a lot of wealth.

Zenobia's queenship was an open, tolerant one. Palmyra was a place full of different languages and religions. **Zenobia herself spoke several languages.** She was known for her beauty, and her love of learning. Her court was full of scholars and philosophers, and she welcomed and protected **people of all religions, cultures, and backgrounds.** There were Greeks, Syrians, and Aramaic people, and Pagan, Christian, and Jewish religions, as well as the native religion of Syria, which involved the worship of the sun god *Bel*. Zenobia's rule was popular, with a good government, and so her people were happy and content.

Queen Zenobia was still ruling as part of the Roman empire – she was only a queen because the Romans accepted her and allowed her to be. Her small empire was known as the *Palmyrene Empire*. But in 270 C.E., the queen did something daring and surprising: **she declared her son, Vaballathus, to be the emperor, and named herself empress of Palmyra.**

In doing this, she was **declaring her independence from Rome,** and that her empire was now free. This did not make the Roman Emperor at all happy! Even more daringly, **Zenobia launched an invasion** to conquer Egypt, which was ruled by Rome. She sent her trusted general, *Zabdas*, to Egypt, and their forces won, **claiming the country for Zenobia.** She then moved to take Palestine and Anatolia (today's Turkey).

These were incredibly brave and daring things to do, given the size and might of Rome. The fact that **Zenobia's forces took each country** they invaded is equally surprising and must have shocked the Roman Emperor. It was a blow to Rome, this swift rebellion – not to mention the loss of Egypt, which along with Palmyra was another source of goods and wealth for them.

The Roman Emperor *Aurelian* had to act swiftly, and he marched out with his army to retake the lost territories. He was just as fierce as Zenobia's forces had been, easily retaking each country. He then surrounded Zenobia's capital city. It's said that letters were exchanged between the two leaders, but in the end Aurelian won and **Zenobia was forced to surrender.** She was taken to Rome to be paraded in a public display by the emperor in his triumph and victory. This was a common punishment for those defeated by Rome.

No one knows what happened to Zenobia after the victory parade – however, many stories say that she was allowed to live, and that she lived out the rest of her days in Rome. Despite being captured, Zenobia's courage and daring in going against the largest empire of the time was something very few rulers would have done, as they feared what would happen to them. Today, in her homeland of Syria, 1,800 years after her rule, Zenobia is not only remembered but honoured, hailed as a national symbol.

> ### INTERESTING FACT:
> Zenobia, like Boudicca and Amanirenas before her, was a female ruler who had the courage to pit herself against the Roman Empire. She was remarkable for the tolerant court she ruled, accepting people of all places and religions, and encouraging musicians, mathematicians, scholars, and philosophers across her empire.

HYPATIA
(Hi-pay-sha)

Lived: 370 C.E. - 415 C.E.
Location: Alexandria, Egypt
Occupation: Mathematician, Philosopher

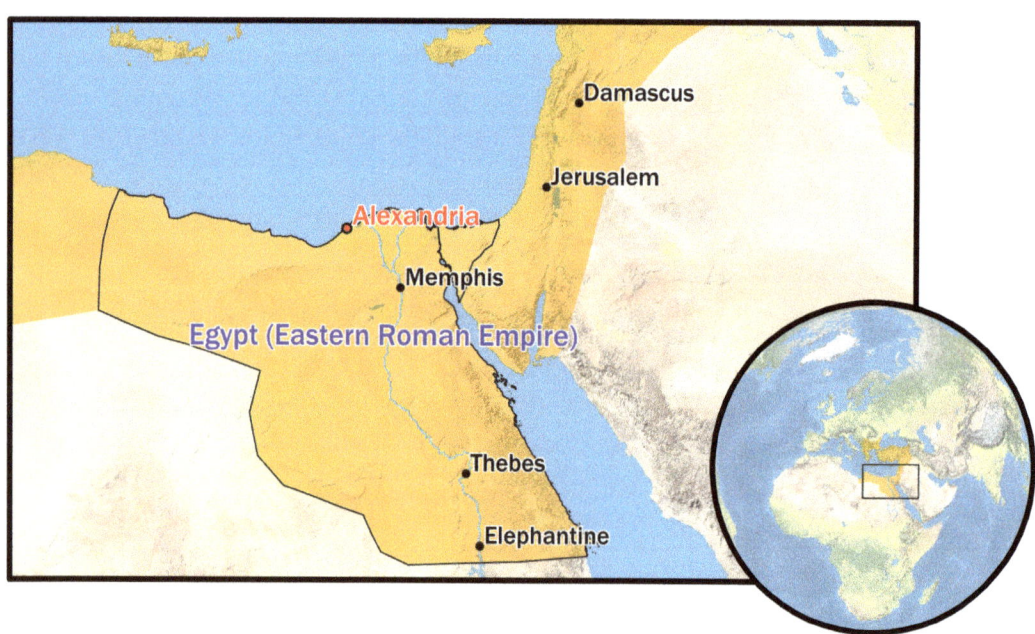

Hypatia was a woman of towering intellect. In a world where men were the scholars and politicians, and women were wives who stayed at home, Hypatia learnt mathematics and astronomy from her father.

Alexandria was a big city in Egypt, which was a nation ruled by the *Roman Empire*. Egyptians, Romans, and Greeks all lived here. It was an **important place for trade and learning.** The fourth century was an interesting time here as there was political upheaval, with Christians of the time gaining influence but opposed by those who were still Pagans. Christians believed in one God, and Pagans believed in the many gods of Rome and Greece. These different beliefs caused problems, as each faction wanted to govern Alexandria in their own way.

Most women in the city, like elsewhere in the Greek and Roman world, were not well educated and did not engage in politics or learning. In fact, women were expected only to walk around in public places if they had a man of their family with them – their father or brother if they were not yet married, or their husband if they were married.

Hypatia was Greek. Her father was a man of learning, and he gave his daughter **an education in mathematics, astronomy, and philosophy** – all subjects that were respected in Alexandria and beyond. Hypatia was clever, and she learned quickly. When she grew up, she was so well educated and so clever that she was able to discuss these subjects with educated men. **Hypatia became a teacher of philosophy and maths** – an incredible achievement for a woman in the Ancient Greek world.

*This object is called an **astrolabe**, it is a scientific tool that is used to find stars, tell time, and help travellers know where they are.*

Hypatia is known to have made astrolabes, as well as other scientific instruments. She also wrote a great deal about mathematics!

In 400 C.E., **Hypatia became the head** of the *Platonist School*, which was a school at which men could learn and discuss philosophy, mathematics, medicine, and astronomy. People came from far and wide **to listen to Hypatia talk** on these subjects. Many respected and indeed admired her, for her intellect and the work that she was doing in these subjects. She even had the respect of politicians, and she was known to advise them and give them counsel. Hypatia did not marry, instead continuing to teach and work in the academic fields.

In government, the arguments between Pagans and Christians were reaching a crisis point: the Pagans held the most power, but the Christians were gaining influence and wanted to change things. Hypatia herself was a Pagan, but she tolerated all people of all faiths and beliefs. **She valued knowledge and learning** above political and religious views, and her students came from all backgrounds.

> ### INTERESTING FACT:
> Before Hypatia, there was a female mathematician called Pandrosion. She lived just before Hypatia and developed new mathematical methods of calculation. So Hypatia was not the only woman working in academic fields, although she was one of very, very few that we know of today. Perhaps there were more, but their stories have not been recorded… Who knows?

The Christian political leaders, however, did not like a woman talking to learned men or teaching. It was wrong, they said, and **demanded that she give up her position.** But Hypatia ignored them, refusing their demands, determined to continue teaching and studying astronomy and mathematics.

Sadly, the political arguments of the two factions soon boiled over and turned into fighting. The whole city was engulfed, with many people taking sides. There were riots and fires broke out. In the chaos, Hypatia was killed. None of her written work has survived. A philosopher of the time named *Socrates* (a different Socrates to the *very* famous philosopher), described Hypatia as:

> *"[Having] made such attainments in literature and science, as to far surpass all the philosophers of her own time… For all men on account of her extraordinary dignity and virtue admired her the more."*

AL-KHANSA
(Al-Kan-za)

Lived: 575 C.E. - 646 C.E.
Location: Arabia
Occupation: Poet

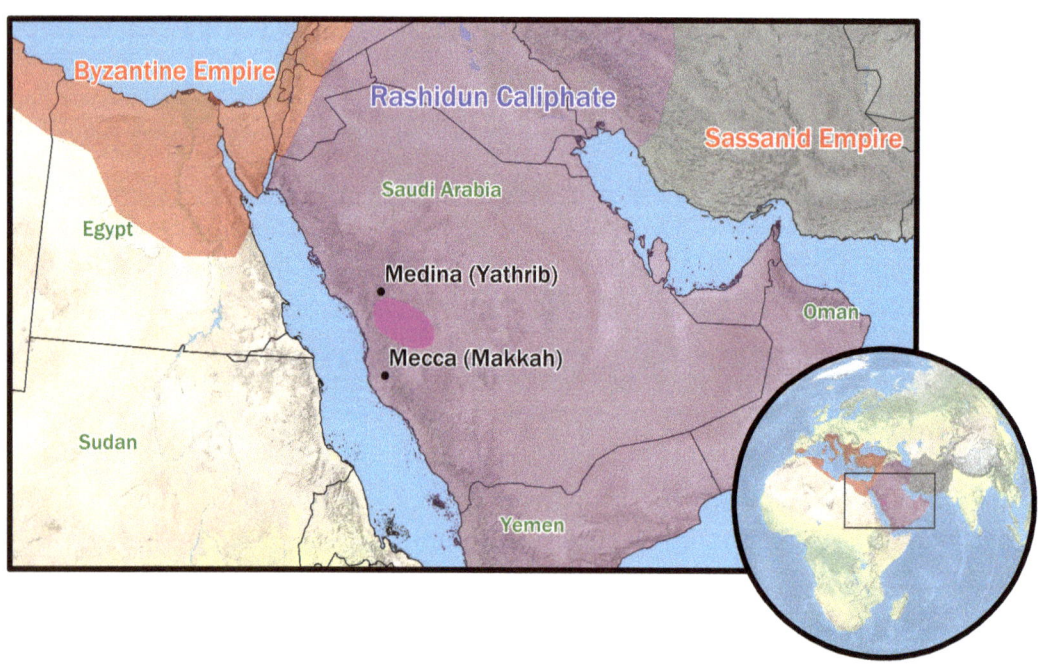

Al-Khansa lived 1,500 years ago, at the same time as the Muslim prophet Muhammad. Al-Khansa is famous for her poetry.

A l-Khansa was a nickname, meaning 'snub-nosed.' Her full name was Tumadir bint Amr ibn al-Harith ibn al-Sharid al-Sulamiyah. During her lifetime in Arabia, **female poets were common,** because it was the duty of women to write elegies for the dead.

> ### INTERESTING FACT:
> An 'elegy' is special poem to mourn those who have died.

At this time in Arabia, **people lived in tribes.** Tribes were groups of people that lived in the same area and who shared beliefs and customs. There were many different tribes in Arabia, and each could be thousands of people, or much smaller. Al-Khansa, daughter of the chief, was of the *Banu Sulaym* nomadic tribe, who moved around rather than living in one place. **She lived at the time of the Prophet Muhammad,** who was teaching the religion of Islam. Most nomadic Arabians in this pre-Islamic time believed in many gods, and some were Jewish or Christian.

For the pre-Islamic tribes, elegies for the dead were important. At certain times, the tribes would all come together in a big gathering and have poetry competitions. Al-Khansa's poetry was mostly in praise of her father and her brothers, all of whom had died in battle. **She wrote over 100 poems** about her brothers in particular, whom she had loved very much and missed greatly.

At the gatherings, all the **women would stand and speak their own poems**, and then all would agree on whose was the best. Al-Khansa performed her sad poems in these competitions, and she was so good that **she won great respect and fame across Arabia.** She is unique in her status as the best-known female poet of her time.

In the year 629 C.E., **al-Khansa's tribe travelled to meet the Prophet Muhammad** and hear him speak about Allah, the one God. When al-Khansa met the prophet, he asked to hear her poems, and when she recited them, he found them so beautiful and powerful that he wept. It is said that **al-Khansa was his favourite poet.** After meeting the prophet, al-Khansa converted to Islam. She married and had six children, all of whom also became poets.

There is a story that says a male poet told al-Khansa that she was "the greatest [female] poet," to which she responded, **"I am the greatest poet [of all]"**! Today, almost 1,000 lines of her poetry remain. Her collected poems have been published in a book called *The Diwan*, and it has been translated into English.

Here are some beautiful lines from al-Khansa's poetry:

> *"O my eyes, shed generous tears,*
>
> *Weep for Sakhr the generous*
>
> *Cry for your brave brother..."*

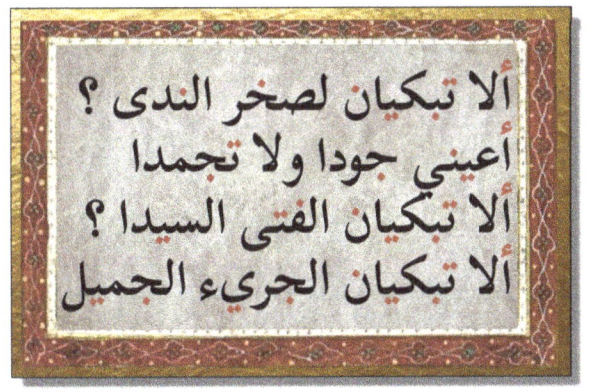

Here is the same part of Al-Khansa's poem in the style of classical Arabic calligraphy.

INTERESTING FACT:

Al-Khansa's poems were spoken in her native Arabian language, and they would have sounded very different than they do in English. Poetry can be difficult to translate, because it can lose its rhythm and meaning when it is changed into a different language.

Wu Zetian
(Woo Zer-tee-en)

Lived: 624 C.E. - 705 C.E.
Location: China
Occupation: Empress

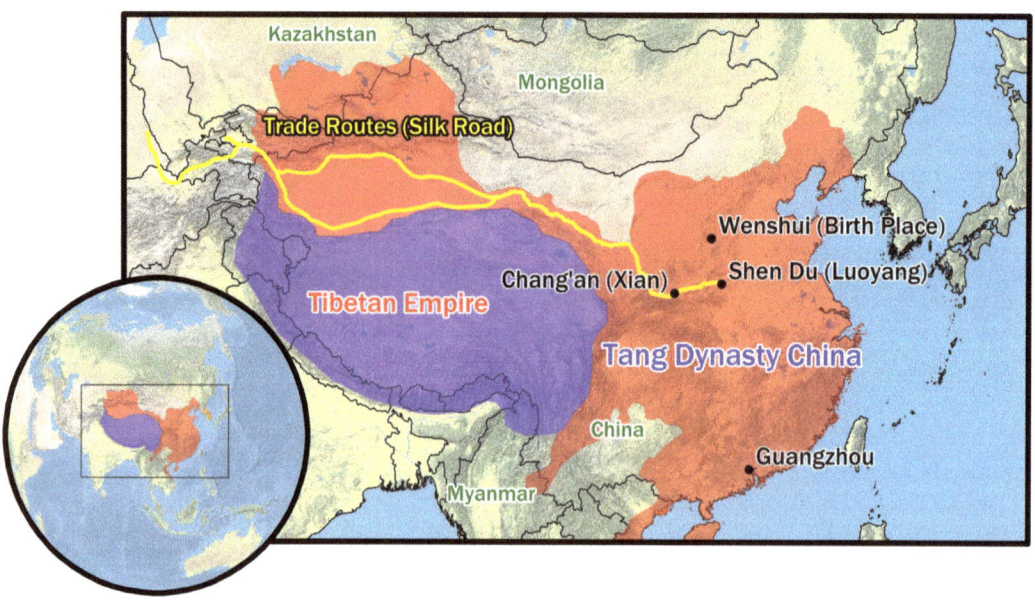

Wu Zetian is famous through history because she was the only empress of China to rule in her own name. Although there were other empresses, they all ruled on behalf of their sons, but Lady Wu took the throne and the title for herself.

Wu Zetian, also known as Wu Zhao and Lady Wu, started life as a noblewoman, born to a wealthy family. Unusually for a woman of her time in China, she was well educated – **she could read, write, and knew about political affairs.** By age fourteen, she had been taken into the royal household to read poetry to the emperor. When the emperor died, his son replaced him and became *Emperor Gaozong.* He fell in love with Wu, and they married.

When her husband the emperor was quite ill, **he passed his decision-making on to Wu.** She ruled with the authority of an emperor, able to make important decisions and enact policies. Gaozong died in 683 C.E., and it was usual for the wife of an emperor to retire after the death of her husband – but not Wu Zetian. Her son took the throne but, ambitious and determined, **Wu deposed him** after only two months. She put herself in charge on her younger son's behalf. Before he could rule, however, **Wu declared herself empress** and sent both her sons into exile, to live far away from the court.

Empress Wu did everything she could to eliminate any threat to her power – from her own family, from other nobles, and from anyone else who opposed her. It was against tradition for a woman to rule, so there were many who wanted to get rid of her. They wanted one of her sons or another man of the noble class to be emperor instead. But Wu was very clever and ruthless. She appointed people who were only loyal to her into important government positions. She also set up a **network of secret spies**, who would be able to warn her of any complaints and rebellions. She exiled anyone who even thought of speaking out against her.

> ### INTERESTING FACT:
> Empress Wu changed her name: having several names was common in Chinese culture, and emperors often took a different name upon rising to the throne. She declared her name as 'Zhou,' founding the Zhou Dynasty.

The **common people loved the empress,** because she listened to them and made changes that made life easier for them. China had a strict hierarchy, and the peasants – those who did not come from noble upper-class families – were rarely thought about by those in charge. But Wu added laws and rules that made life better for commoners. She allowed people from **humble**

backgrounds to take the exams to become government officials, something that had never been done before. **Empress Wu ruled over a time of peace** for her empire, and her people were content. But the upper class did not like the reforms she put in place.

> ### INTERESTING FACT:
>
> To work for the government, people in China had to take exams. If they passed, they were allowed to work in the civil service – i.e. working for the government. How well they did in those exams determined what job they got, and how important that job was.

Empress Wu was a Buddhist and she gave money to Buddhist monasteries. This made her popular with Buddhists, but unpopular with those who followed other religions. She also **opened up trade routes,** including the famous *Silk Road*, which allowed more goods to flow into China from other countries and places. Not only was she ruthless in getting rid of her enemies, but she was also good at putting laws into place that brought the common folk on to her side. She was a great strategist and **she expanded her empire** successfully, gaining more land and territory. She also dealt with threats from Tibet and Korea on China's borders.

In the year 705, having ruled for twenty-two years, Empress Wu was getting old and suffering from ill health. She had trusted people around her more and more, but they had become corrupt, serving only themselves with their power. The noble court, having had enough of the bad behaviour of these officials, **finally forced empress Wu to abdicate** the throne in favour of her exiled son, *Zhongzong*. Lady Wu left court, and she died shortly afterwards.

> ### INTERESTING FACT:
>
> Emperor Zhongzong was a weak ruler and his wife, Wei, took control of all his power. She only ruled for seventeen days before being overthrown and removed from power by her nephew, who then became emperor.

Aethelflaed
(Ee-thul-fled)

Lived: 869 C.E. - 918 C.E.
Location: Mercia, England
Occupation: Lady of the Mercians

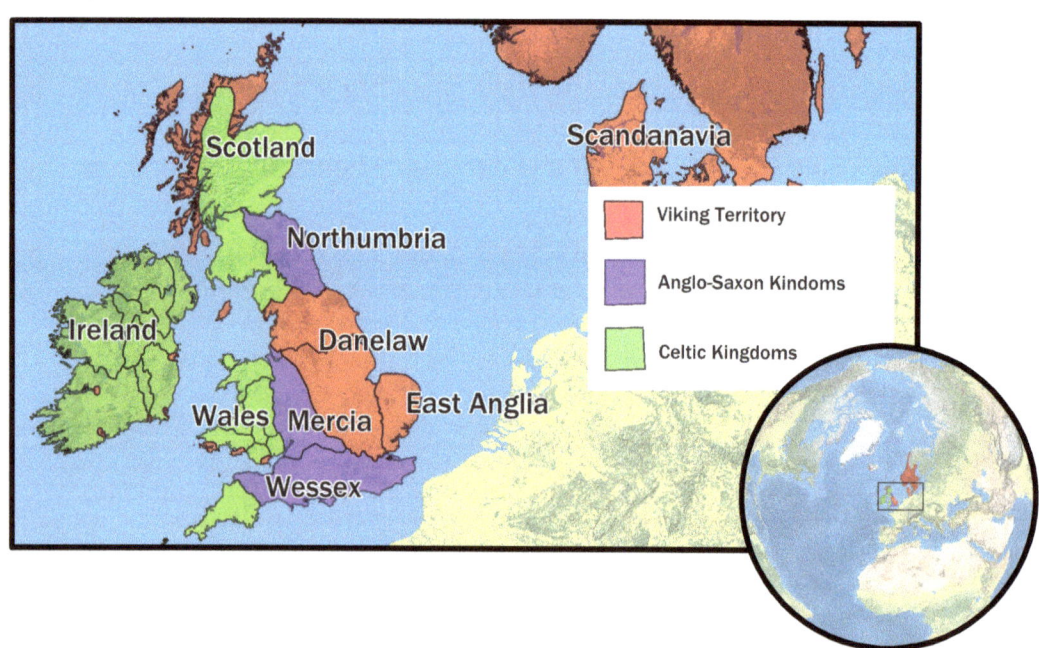

Aethelflaed was the daughter of King Alfred the Great, and she played a very important role in creating England as we know it today. She was a powerful figure for her time and country.

In 869 C.E., England as a whole country did not exist: instead, there were **several kingdoms**, each with its own king. The people living in England at this time were known as the *Anglo-Saxons*.

Aethelflaed was the eldest child of *King Alfred*. She lived during the time when *Vikings* were raiding Britain, taking land and settling. These invaders were warriors from Denmark, Sweden, and Norway. Aethelflaed grew up watching her father trying to negotiate peace, going to battle, and fortifying towns with stronger walls and more soldiers. But **the Vikings had taken much of England**, installing their own chiefs and creating the *Danelaw* in Northumbria, East Anglia, and a portion of Mercia. Only Wessex, the home of King Alfred, and a smaller part of Mercia remained in Anglo-Saxon control.

INTERESTING FACTS:

The term 'Viking' comes from 'Vikingr', which actually meant 'to go raiding'. Most of the Vikings who settled in England came from Denmark and were Pagans, believing in many gods (The Anglo-Saxons were Christians). The 'Danelaw' were the customs and laws of the Pagan Danish people who took over the land, and were different to the laws of the Anglo-Saxon English.

Aethelflaed was educated, thanks to her father, which was extremely unusual – girls were not given an education at this time. King Alfred valued learning, and so his daughter learned the same subjects as her brother, *Edward*. In 886, Aethelflaed married *Lord Aethelred* of Mercia. This **ensured a strong alliance** between the only English rulers left in the country. Aethelflaed was half Mercian, as her mother came from Mercia, so the people of Mercia were overjoyed to welcome her as their noble Lady.

Only a few short years later, with her husband suffering illness, **Aethelflaed was making decisions** and taking decisive action to try and prevent Viking raids on her lands. She created a fort at Chester, and when it was attacked in a raid, she sent her army to push the invaders back. Not only that, but she managed to talk to one group of Vikings and **convince them to switch to her side,** so that they then joined her army instead!

King Alfred died in 899, and his son Edward became king of Wessex, continuing to battle against the Vikings. He and Aethelred and Aethelflaed were often allies, fighting for the survival of their Christian, Anglo-Saxon kingdom. In 911, Aethelred died. The council of Mercia voted overwhelmingly for **Aethelflaed to continue as the ruler of Mercia.** This was extraordinary – for a woman to rule on her own. It had never been done before! Aethelflaed became known as **'the Lady of the Mercians'.** She never took the title of 'queen,' because her brother was king of Wessex and wanted to be the king of all the English, which had been his father's dream.

This is a picture of a coin that was minted in Mercia during the reign of Aethelflaed.

Aethelflaed was tough, clever, and determined. **She ordered towns to be fortified** across her borders, and for new towns to be built. Thanks to the education that she had received as well as studying her father's strategies, she knew what to do to keep the Vikings at bay. These **fortifications prevented the enemy** from being able to run deep into her lands, as they would be seen by those in the border towns, and a force of soldiers would always be on hand to fight back.

Aethelflaed was not content with this, though: **she led her army in person** (though she did not fight) and travelled to Derby, a Viking controlled city that was important as a trading centre. She ordered her army to attack the city – and they won. In the following year, 918, the major **Viking city of Leicester actually surrendered to Aethelflaed!** Her reputation must have been enormous for these fierce, battle-hardened warriors to simply hand over the city to her without a fight!

In the same year, shortly after her success with Leicester, **the city of York agreed to terms** with Aethelflaed. This was another huge victory, and it would have seen the whole of the country firmly back under English Christian rule (Aethelflaed's brother had been busy in the south of the country and had taken back East Anglia from the Vikings.) Sadly, though, Aethelflaed fell ill, and died before she could finalise the treaty with York. But she had done so much to change the balance of power between the Vikings and the Anglo-Saxons that her legacy would live on after her.

Because of his sister's hard work, King Edward was able to gain more territory than the Anglo-Saxons had ever had since the Vikings first arrived on British shores.

Aethelflaed's daughter, *Aelfwynn*, was the heir to Mercia, and it is the **only instance** in early history of a rulership **passing from mother to daughter.** Aelfwynn only ruled for a few months though before her uncle, King Edward, took Mercia for his own. Some say that he took the land by force, deposing Aelfwynn, and some think it was by agreement with the Mercian council as they wanted a strong ruler... We will never know the truth. But what we do know is that Aethelflaed was much loved and respected by her own people *and* the Vikings, and she is remembered as a heroine today for her bravery, her courage, and her cleverness in outfoxing her enemies.

After King Edward died, his son *Aethelstan* became king. As a youth, Aethelstan had been **sent to Mercia** to be looked after by his aunt Aethelflaed, and it was she who oversaw his education and training. As the king, Aethelstan continued his family's fight and legacy, and eventually claimed full victory over the Vikings. He was the **first king to be known as 'the king of all the English'** – the whole country, at last, was ruled by a single king. He had his aunt Aethelflaed to thank for helping to make this dream happen.

INTERESTING FACTS:

In 672 C.E., 240 years before Aethelflaed, records name another woman as ruling in her own right after the death of her husband: Seaxburh, wife of King Ceanwalh. However, she only ruled for two years and was deposed in 674 C.E. by a rival branch of the royal family.

In 722 C.E., Aethelburh, married to King Ine, led a military campaign without her husband and won, destroying Taunton (in the south-west of the country). She never ruled in her own right, though.

Hroswitha
(Hoss-veet-a)

Lived: 935 C.E. - 973 C.E.
Location: Gandersheim, Saxony
Occupation: Nun, Playwright

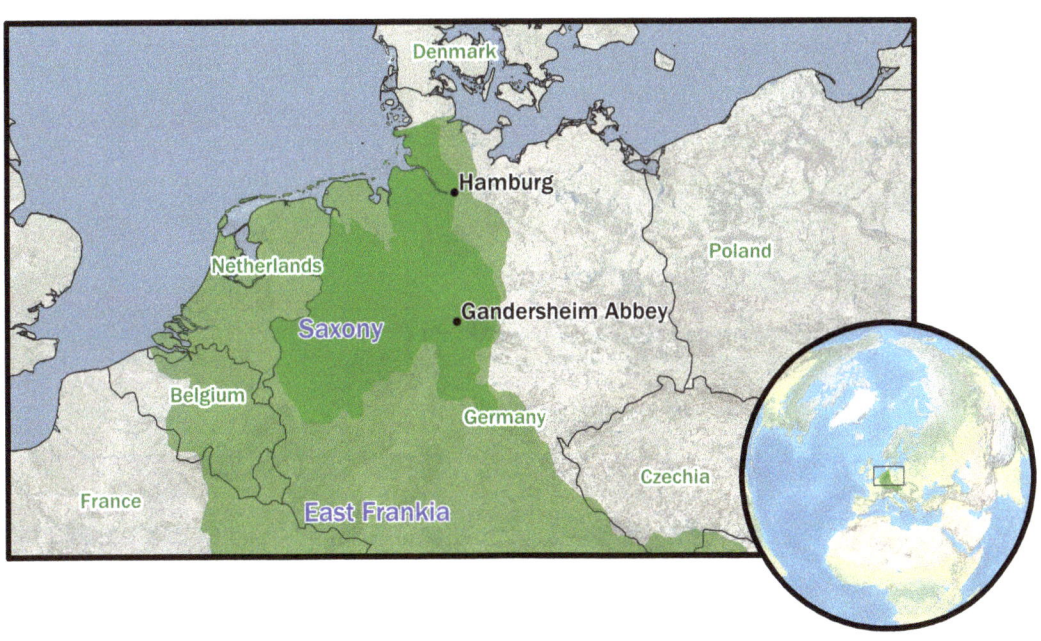

Hroswitha was a Christian nun who lived in Gandersheim, Saxony – today's northern Germany. She is famous for writing poetry and plays. Nuns lived in convents and led a simple life of contemplation and being devoted to God.

Hroswitha was **educated in reading and writing**, which was highly unusual for a woman in the 900s. She had chosen to become a nun and live in a convent. This was a special place where only nuns lived together, praying, farming, gardening, and leading a simple life.

Because she could read and write, **Hroswitha chose to spend her time writing plays.** This was a response to other written plays of the time, which were all by men, and they showed women as weak and not able to do much, incapable of thinking as cleverly as men! Hroswitha was so angry about this that she wrote her own plays to show that women were not weak, and that they too were able to have a connection to God, and overcome challenges. As well as writing **comedy plays in Latin, Hroswitha also wrote poetry.**

Why is this important? Because Hroswitha is known as **the first German female writer, historian, and poet!** She was the very first woman in Germany to write plays and poems. She led the way for other women to do so and showed that it was not only men who should be allowed to write! She was also the very first person in northern Europe to write about Islam. Her plays were legends and comedies, centred on her Christian faith. But she only shared them with her sister nuns.

Hroswitha's plays were lost to history for a long time, and they were only rediscovered around the year 1500, over 500 years after her life! She also **wrote about her life** during the Middle Ages, making her one of the only people who recorded the everyday life of women of that time. Most written work was about important men. This record of women's lives is incredibly useful to historians, to better understand what life was like for women during this time. Her work has been translated into different languages and can still be read today.

INTERESTING FACTS:

Another famous German nun lived just over 100 years after Hroswitha. Hildegard of Bingen, who was born in 1098 and died in 1179, was famous for writing and composing. She was also a philosopher, and medical practitioner! She wrote many songs which are still in existence today.

FREYDIS EIRIKSDOTTIR
(Fray-dis Ay-rics-dot-teer)

Lived: 965 C.E. - unknown
Location: Iceland
Occupation: Explorer

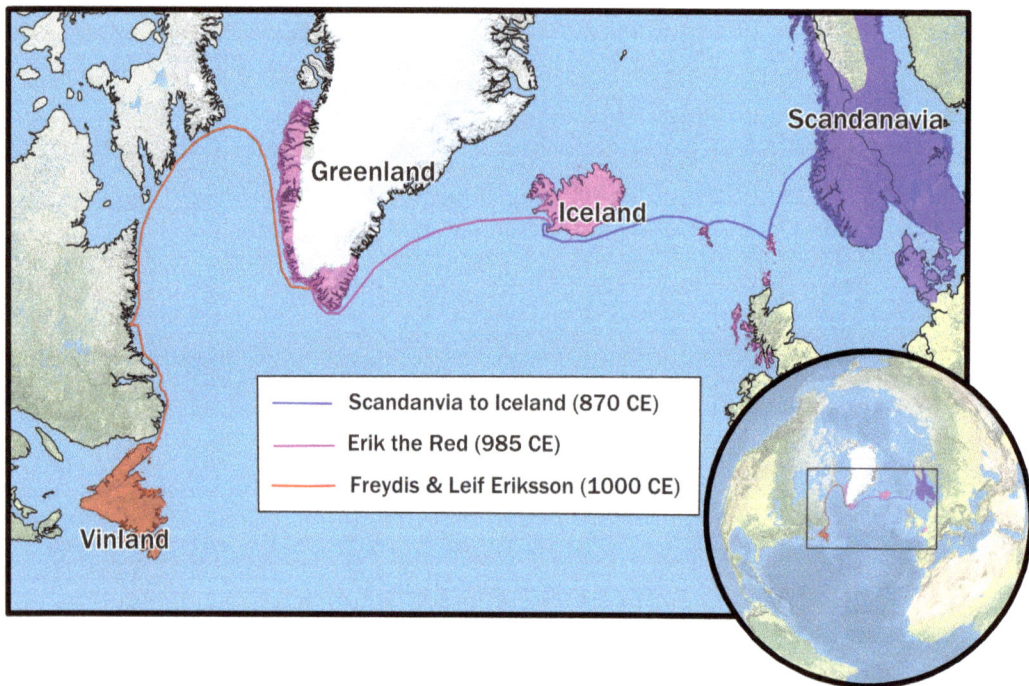

Freydis was a Norse woman who lived during the time of the Vikings. The Norse people were from Scandinavia and Iceland, and they were known to be fierce warriors and adventurous explorers, who used their longships to navigate seas and raid other countries.

reydis' father was *Erik the Red*, who was a famous explorer. Erik came from Iceland, which was very new as a discovered country, and had only been settled by people about 100 years before Freydis' lifetime.

Erik was exiled from Iceland for committing a crime. He was forced to leave the country, so he went exploring. He landed on a wild and empty land, which was completely uninhabited. It was cold and barren, but Erik had a plan. **He named the country Greenland** and he decided to make it his home. Eventually he went back to Iceland to convince other people to follow him and settle there.

INTERESTING FACT:

He named the new place 'Greenland', to convince others to move and settle there, though it was very cold and empty! 'Greenland' sounds much more enticing than 'Coldland' or 'Emptyplace'! People must have been quite surprised, and maybe a little cross, when they found out that it was not, in fact, green!

Freydis had a brother, *Leif Erikson*, who was known as 'Leif the Lucky.' He also liked exploring, and he was **the first European to land on the American continent.** This was hundreds of years before Columbus discovered America (although of course there were people already living there: the Native Americans, or First Nation peoples). Leif named the area that he explored *Vinland*, which was a small part of the continent, on the coast. He did not stay there, though, and after a while he went back home.

So, Freydis came from a family of adventurers and explorers. After her brother's long journey to and from Vinland, **Freydis decided that she wanted to join in with the adventures**. She demanded that she got to go to Vinland, too, so her brother provided her with a ship and everything that she would need for the long journey and her stay whilst she was there.

Every journey at this time would have been dangerous in a wooden longship, with no shelter from the weather or storms. It took many weeks or even months to travel to other countries. Lots of ships would travel together, and often some of them would be lost to the sea, never reaching their destination.

Freydis was determined, though, and she brought men with her on the journey, to explore and to try to find valuables they could take back home. We know about Freydis and her expedition to Vinland from two Scandinavian sagas (stories, or accounts): *Saga of the Greenlanders* and *Saga of Erik the Red.*

Each saga gives a slightly different tale of Freydis. She and her people made it across the dangerous Atlantic Ocean, reaching their destination safely. They set up camp, and **spent about a year there,** exploring the local area.

However, it was not a happy group. Freydis and the other leaders argued a lot, and these arguments turned violent. The two groups clashed, and the other leaders were killed. Later, the camp was attacked by the native people of the land, who the Vikings called *Skraelings*. Freydis' men were **so scared by these fearsome foes** that they flung down their weapons and ran away. Freydis, furious with her men, picked up a sword and shouted at her companions, calling them cowards. She turned to face the enemy, brandishing the sword and shouting at them. She must have looked very fierce, because **they ran away** from her!

Vinland was never fully settled by the Norse, and the colonies did not stay there. It was not until hundreds of years later that 'America' became a settled country by Europeans... but of course native American peoples had already been there for a long, long time.

Nothing further is known of Freydis, as all we have are the sagas that record her adventures. But she was certainly a very brave woman who wasn't afraid of a challenge or the unknown.

INTERESTING FACT:

Gudrid Thorbjarnardottir was another Icelandic woman who, in 980 C.E. went to Vinland. She is also mentioned in the Sagas. She married Leif's brother – so she was the sister-in-law of Freydis. Her husband died, and Gudrid remarried, to a man called Thorfin. They travelled together to Vinland with many others in an attempt to settle the place, and Gudrid had a son - the first European to be born there. However, they too encountered the native people, and eventually left Vinland due to ongoing fights and raids.

Murasaki Shikibu

(Mura-sar-ki She-kee-boo)

Lived: 973 C.E. - 1014 C.E., possibly later
Location: Japan
Occupation: Author

Murasaki Shikibu was a Japanese noblewoman, who became famous for writing something very special.

Murasaki was born in Japan to a wealthy family. **She was well educated**, and she was so clever that she learned Chinese, against all the rules of the time. Only boys were allowed to learn Chinese, as this was the language that educated men wrote in. **Defying tradition,** Murasaki listened in on her brother's lessons and was very good at learning fast.

Murasaki later married and had a daughter, but her husband died just a few years after she was born. With her young daughter, Murasaki went to the royal court where her father worked and was employed by the empress, *Shoshi*. Here, **Murasaki wrote poetry and diaries**, which was a normal pastime for ladies of the court. But Murasaki did something else that was extraordinary: she wrote a book, titled *The Tale of Genji*.

Her novel is special because it is considered the **very first novel ever written!** No one else had ever written a long, made-up story with imaginary characters in a book! Writing documents had been around for a very long time, and the Ancient Romans and Greeks wrote plays and poems. The first story had been written over 1,000 years ago in Mesopotamia (*The Epic of Gilgamesh*), but this was written as a series of poems and was based on a real person. Folk tales (myths and legends) were known, and Murasaki enjoyed reading these. But a long story, entirely made up and imaginary, telling of ordinary people doing ordinary things – this had never been done before!

The Tale of Genji is about life at court, featuring elegant people, and the life and loves of a prince. **It is still available today to read,** and it is still loved by people in Japan – a legacy that has lasted for over 1,000 years! The book is twice as long as *War and Peace*, written in 1867, which is famous for being a very long story indeed. Murasaki's novel spreads over more than 100 years and has over 400 characters in it – quite an accomplishment for the first novel ever! It was written in *kana* – Japanese writing.

Murasaki also wrote a collection of 128 poems in her lifetime. Her diary tells us that she did not enjoy life at court, as she complained often of the people there (perhaps this is why she spent so much time writing!)

Murasaki's novel was widely known in Japan within ten years of it being completed, and within one hundred years, **it was a classic of Japanese literature.** *The Tale of Genji* was not translated into English until 1933 – that's 1,000 years after it was written!

The name Murasaki Shikibu is not the author's real name – in fact, there is no record of her true name.

The end of her life, where and how she lived out her days, and when exactly Murasaki died are not known. But to write the very first novel in the world has earned her a name to be remembered.

INTERESTING FACTS:

Murasaki lived during the Heian period of Japan. Courtly women were not referred to by their given names, but instead by titles related to themselves or their male relatives. 'Murasaki' is the term for the colour violet, and there is a piece of art of her dressed in a violet robe.

Murasaki's daughter, Kenshi, also wrote poetry. She wrote about thirty-eight poems, and these too have survived to this day.

Emma of Normandy

Lived: 984 C.E. - 1052 C.E.
Location: England
Occupation: Queen

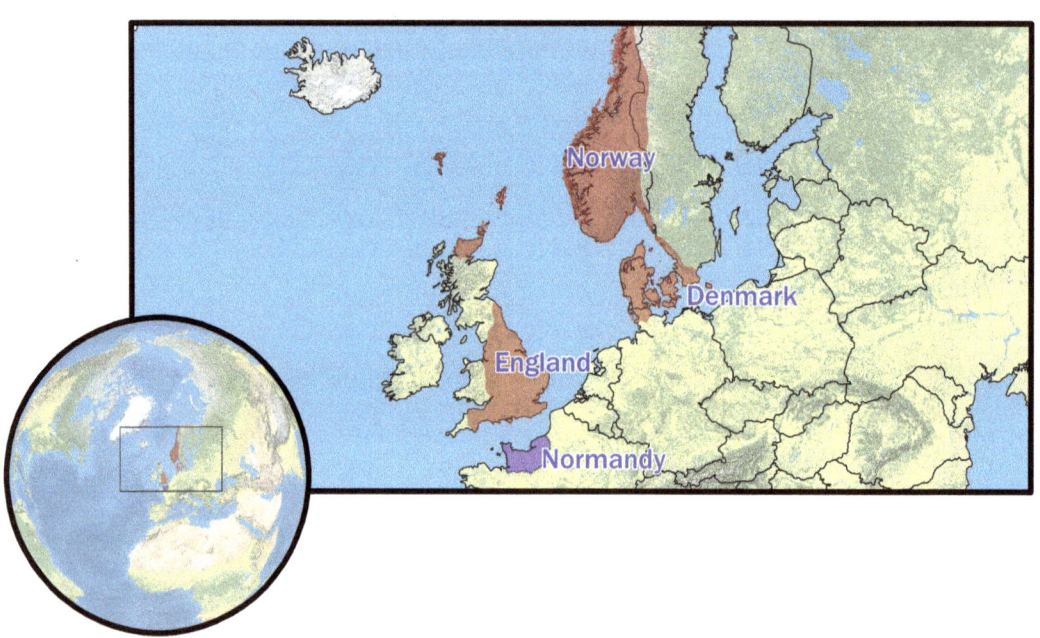

Emma of Normandy lived in a chaotic time, when the throne of England was fought over and changed hands frequently. She became queen of not one but three countries! Her actions had important consequences for the future of England...

Emma was born in Normandy, France, and was the daughter of a duke named *Richard*. In 1002, she married *king Aethelred* of England. On the day of her marriage, Emma was given an Anglo-Saxon name: *Aelfgifu*. (The Anglo-Saxons were the people of England at that time, and their names can sound very different and strange from the names that we have today.)

> ### INTERESTING FACTS:
> Repeated names can be confusing! THIS Aethelred and Emma come about seventy years after Aethelflaed and Aethelred, who you have already read about. 'Aethelred' was clearly a popular royal name!

Emma was also given many estates across the south of England, and the city of Exeter! This made her incredibly wealthy, and she used this wisely, managing her estates so well that she continued to increase her own personal wealth. She became known as **the richest woman in England!** She and Aethelred had three children: *Edward, Alfred,* and a daughter, *Godgifu*. Aethelred had been married before and already had several children before he married Emma. (All of these children become quite important later on, as you will see).

In 1013, **England was invaded** by *Sweyn Forkbeard* from Denmark. He fought and took the throne of England. Aethelred, Emma, and their children **fled the country** in fear for their lives, returning to her homeland of Normandy. However, Sweyn died a year later, and Emma and her husband were able to return to England and regain the throne.

Then, in 1015, Sweyn's son, *King Cnut* of Denmark, invaded England. He failed to take London, though, which kept the royal family safe. Sadly, King Aethelred died in 1016. (A lot happened in a couple of years, didn't it?) **Queen Emma kept control of London** for a short while, while her stepson *Edmund* (who was Aethelred's oldest surviving son) fought with Cnut for control of England. Neither could gain a victory, and so they agreed to divide the country between them. However, Edmund died shortly after, **leaving Cnut in full control.**

Once again, Emma found herself in a dangerous situation. Being clever and savvy, **she agreed to marry Cnut,** to save herself and also her children from imprisonment or worse by the new king. This marriage ensured she remained in power, but also secured the throne for her children in the future.

As Cnut was king of both Denmark and Norway, **Emma then became queen of these countries as well.** When Cnut went back to Denmark or Norway, Emma ruled in his stead in England. This meant that she had the authority of a king in his absence.

Emma and Cnut had two children together – a boy, *Harthacnut,* and a girl, *Gunhilda.* Cnut also had been married before and had two other sons: *Sweyn* (after his father) and *Harold Harefoot.* When Cnut died in 1035, **again Emma had to flee** the country for her own safety, because once more there was a fight for the throne. Emma's sons fought against Cnut's son, Harefoot, as they all had a claim to the throne. **Harefoot won, becoming king** in 1037. He ruled for several years, but then died in 1040.

Emma remained involved in the politics of England throughout all of the turmoil, using her contacts and influence to try and gain the upper hand for herself and her own children. First **her son Harthacnut became king,** and he ruled for two years. Emma remained active in politics to help Harthacnut. After him, her other son **Edward (known as Edward the Confessor) ruled.** However, Edward restricted his mother's power and wealth, perhaps resenting her status and influence.

Emma left court and lived the rest of her life quietly, away from politics. She lived to the age of seventy and died in 1052. She had survived two invasions, two marriages, seen her sons go to battle, losing and winning in turns, and keeping her family on the throne through her own political influence. It must have been no mean feat, in her time, to survive all of that!

Fourteen years after Emma's death, her son King Edward died. As he did not have any children, the throne was yet again in contest. Emma's great nephew, *Duke William of Normandy* in France, came to England, **claiming a right to the throne through his great aunt Emma.** There were two other contestants for the throne, but William won the fight. He was the famous *William the Conqueror,* victor of the *Battle of Hastings,* 1066. Thanks to Emma's marriage to an English king, William of Normandy had a claim to the throne, and his rule was an important point in history, beginning the Norman period.

INTERESTING FACTS:

In Emma's time, 'England' was mostly a single country and had a single ruler, rather than lots of kings in different parts of the country. England finally had some peace in this era, but there were still occasional Viking invasions – as Sweyn and Cnut here show.

Emma – or Aelfgifu – was arguably the most powerful female ruler England had ever seen, until the reign of Queen Elizabeth I centuries later in 1558 C.E.

William the Conqueror, was the Duke of Normandy and <u>conquered England</u> at the battle of Hastings in 1066. Emma of Normandy was his great-Aunt!

Gwenllian ferch Gruffydd

(Gwen-hh-lian verch Griffith)

Lived: 1097 C.E. - 1136 C.E.
Location: Wales
Occupation: Princess, Warrior

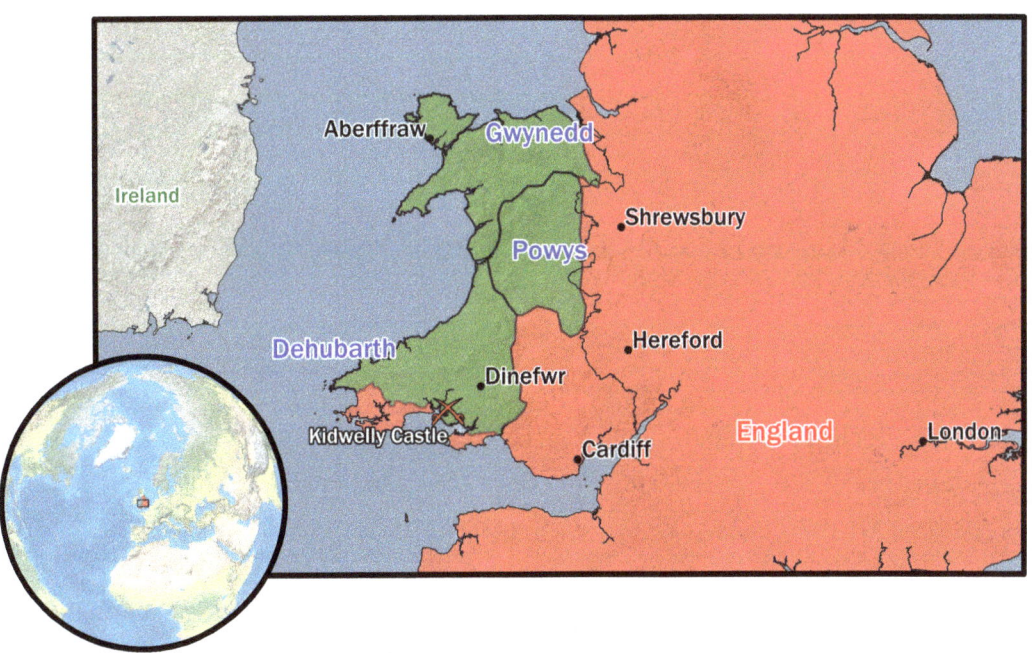

Gwenllian ferch Gruffydd was a Welsh princess who fought against the Normans.

The French Normans had conquered England back in 1066, but Wales had remained an independent country. This was changing, though, with the Normans invading to try and win land. The Welsh, of course, were fighting back, determined to keep themselves free from Norman conquest. Wales at this time was not one unified country with a single ruler, but several kingdoms, each with their own king.

> ### INTERESTING FACTS:
>
> The Welsh language is quite different from English, with different pronunciations. Here's a basic guide to some key sounds:
>
> 'dd' – 'th' as in 'the' or 'than'
>
> 'f' – 'v'
>
> 'ff' – 'f'
>
> 'll' – a hard 'h' sound, or a hiss without the 'ss'
>
> 'ch' – soft, not like in 'church,' but like in 'echo'

Gwenllian lived on the island of Anglesey *(also called Ynys Mon)* in the very north of Wales. She was the youngest daughter of the king of Gwynedd, *Gruffydd ap Cynan*. He had been fighting the Normans for years. As a young woman, Gwenllian met a visiting prince, *Gruffydd ap Rhys*, and they quickly fell in love. They ran away together and married soon afterwards. **The couple lived in the kingdom of Deheubarth** in south Wales, which was a long way from Gwenllian's family home.

South Wales was struggling against the Normans, who were causing trouble there, and Gwenllian and her husband soon had to flee, leaving their home and hiding out by the mountains and in the forests. But Gwenllian did not just hide out and hope her husband would win against their enemy: **she joined Gruffydd ap Rhys in fighting the invaders**, going with him and their men on lightning raids to attack Norman camps and territories. They would harass the enemy, and take what goods and money they could carry, which they then redistributed among their own people (just like Robin Hood!).

Gruffydd left Gwenllian to go and ask her father for his help in the fight against the Normans. He had to travel a long way, as they lived in the south of the country and Gwenllian's father was in the very north. It would have been a tiring journey and a dangerous one, as Gruffydd tried to avoid all enemies.

While he was gone, **the Normans again attacked the Welsh** in Gwenllian's lands. She felt that she had no choice but to raise an army to defend her people. **She marched with them, leading many men,** and they fought the Normans near Kidwelly Castle (known in Welsh as *Castell Cydweli*). Sadly, Gwenllian's forces were defeated, and she was captured and killed by the Normans. However, her brave actions inspired the rest of south Wales to rise up against the Normans, and they won, taking back some of the territories that the Normans controlled.

The field where Gwenllian's forces are believed to have fought is named after her, called *Maes Gwenllian* ('field of Gwenllian'). Gwenllian is often compared to the much earlier female warrior Boudicca, for her bravery and courage in fighting.

This brave woman certainly deserves to be remembered, and to be as famous as Boudicca!

INTERESTING FACTS:

For centuries after the battle that inspired Wales to rise and revolt, Welshman shouted out in battles, "Dial achos Gwenllian!" Which means, "Revenge for Gwenllian!"

Gwenllian's son was Rhys ap Gruffydd. He became the ruler of Deheubarth, and is still known today as one of the most powerful of the Welsh rulers. He managed to take back a lot of his land from the Normans, and campaigned for fifty years, finally dying in battle in 1197. Rhys is a direct ancestor of the royal Tudor line.

Tomoe Gozen

(Tom-o-eh Go-zen)

Lived: 1157 C.E. - unknown
Location: Japan
Occupation: Samurai

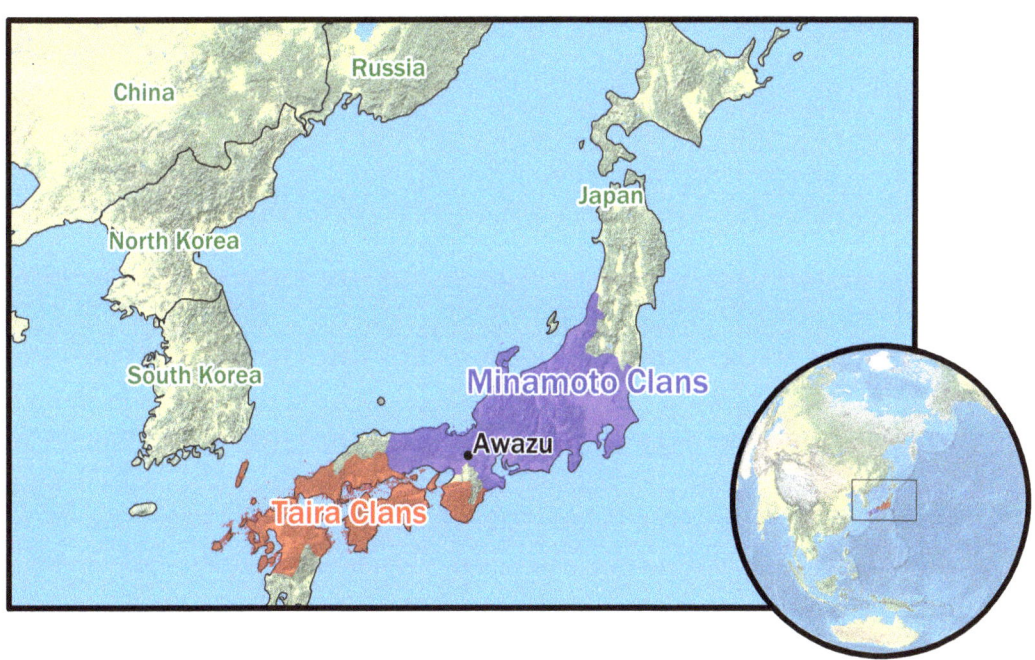

Tomoe was a female samurai who earned a reputation for her bravery.

Tomoe Gozen's exact birth date and early life are unknown, and we only have details of her life as a *samurai*, which was the name given to a **special class of fighters.** Samurai were famous for their dedication, discipline, loyalty, and bravery. There was a long history in Japan of **female samurai,** and they were known as *onna-musha*. Tomoe is one of the most well-known.

Tomoe was skilled at horse riding and in the use of the *naginata*, a long weapon like a spear, as well as the bow. In short, she was exceptional at all skills needed for warfare. In the 1180s, Japan was rife with civil unrest: some of the powerful noble clans wanted to get rid of the emperor, and others were loyal and fought to keep the emperor on the throne. This conflict became a civil war, and it is known as the *Genpei War.*

As a trained onna-musha, **Tomoe fought in the war,** serving under the general *Minamoto no Yoshinaka*, who was fighting against the emperor's forces. Tomoe fought in many battles. She must have been fearless, as she won many fights.

In one such battle, **she led three hundred samurai against an enemy 2,000 strong!** Despite being outnumbered, Tomoe's army won the fight.

At the battle of Awazu, Yoshinaka lost his life, and Tomoe was said to be one of the few warriors who survived. In another battle, Tomoe was influential in her bravery and strategy, **turning the tide** in her side's favour.

The war lasted for five years. Eventually, **Tomoe and the Minamoto forces were victorious.** Yoshinaka's cousin, *Minamoto no Yoritomo* became the *shogun,* 'commander in chief' of Japan, and ruler of the country.

There is no record of what happened to Tomoe Gozen after the war. Her legend was written down in a famous book, *The Tale of the Heike*. She is celebrated as a courageous woman and warrior. Her story also inspired the much later famous female samurai, *Nakano Takeko (see page 164).*

INTERESTING FACTS:

Over the centuries, Japan sometimes had an emperor and sometimes a 'shogun' as their ruler. Japan had many civil wars, with rival clans fighting for control of the country. A shogun was not an emperor, but rather a military commander. The samurai were important and influential in the fight for control as they were the most skilled warriors of their time, and absolutely dedicated to their lords.

The onna-musha were trained just like the men and fought alongside them. There were not just a few – there were many! The onna-musha existed for about 1,000 years in Japan.

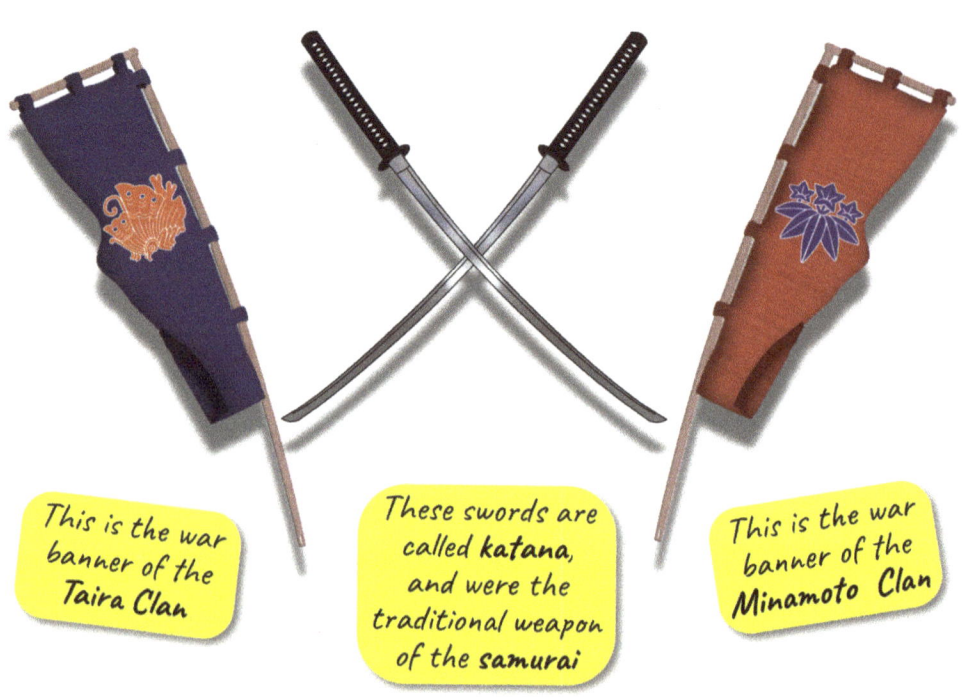

This is the war banner of the **Taira Clan**

These swords are called **katana**, and were the traditional weapon of the **samurai**

This is the war banner of the **Minamoto Clan**

Khutulun
(Kut-oo-yun)

Lived: 1260 C.E. - 1306 C.E.
Location: Central Asia
Occupation: Wrestler, Warrior

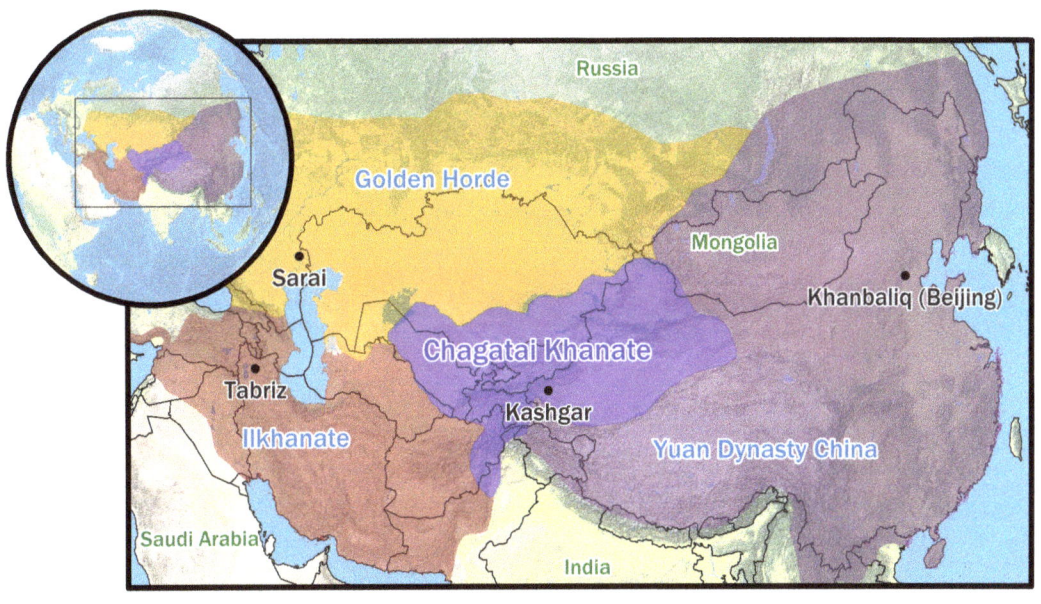

Khutulun was the daughter of Kaidu Khan, the ruler of central Asia. She was a great-great-granddaughter of the famous Genghis Khan, who had conquered a lot of Asia a few generations before.

Khutulun's people were nomadic: they travelled across the country by horse, and they lived in yurts (big tents). They were **expert horse riders** and particularly skilled with the bow. They were famous for shooting their arrows from horseback. Khutulun's father, *Kaidu Khan*, was the chief of their clan.

The people of Asia lived in tribes at this time, and the different tribes often fought one another. Years before Khutulun, her great-great-grandfather, *Genghis Khan,* had united many of the tribes through warfare and conquest, becoming a supreme leader. However, after his death, the old rivalries resurfaced and the tribes began to split again.

Khutulun rode to war alongside her father, fearlessly fighting their enemies. The famous explorer *Marco Polo* (an Italian who travelled across Asia) wrote about her, describing her as a **"superb warrior"** who was able to **easily capture her enemies.** She even fought against her cousin, the great *Kublai Khan*, who was a ruler of another tribe. He ruled from North China and he took on Chinese customs and ways of doing things, which were very different from the traditional Mongolian way of life. This angered Khutulun's father, Kaidu, which caused a rift between the clans, that spilled into a war. Although Kaidu had many sons, he **relied on Khutulun for military advice** and strategy.

> ### INTERESTING FACT:
> Khutulun and her father were of the Chagatai tribe. Her cousin Kublai founded the Yuan Dynasty, and he followed the Chinese way of life and Chinese customs. There were also the Khanates of the Golden Horde, and the Ilkhanate. The Kaidu-Kublai war, as it is known, lasted for thirty-three years.

Khutulun was so great a warrior and so smart at strategy, in fact, that **her father wished to name her as his successor.** However, Kaidu's sons (Khutulun's brothers) rejected this, because it was not customary for women to be leaders. They refused to support her – though this was most likely actually because each of them wanted to be the chief instead – and she never came to rule.

Khutulun was as **talented at wrestling** as she was at being a warrior. In wrestling, Khutulun was better than many men. There were three skills in the Mongolian culture that were highly regarded: horse riding, archery, and wrestling. The stories say that Khutulun was so skilled at wrestling that she demanded **any man who wished to marry her must defeat her**. If they lost, they had to give her horses, which were prized by her people, or wealth. Many men took up her challenge – **and all lost!** In this way, through her prowess at wrestling, she won a great fortune in both herds and wealth.

Khutulun lived to the age of about forty-five, but how she died is not known. Mongolian princess, warrior, and wrestler… Khutulun stands in history as a fierce heroine of her people.

Wrestling, called 'bokh' is still the most popular national sport in Mongolia, along with horse racing and archery

Julian of Norwich

Lived: 1343 C.E. - 1416 C.E.
Location: England
Occupation: Nun, Writer

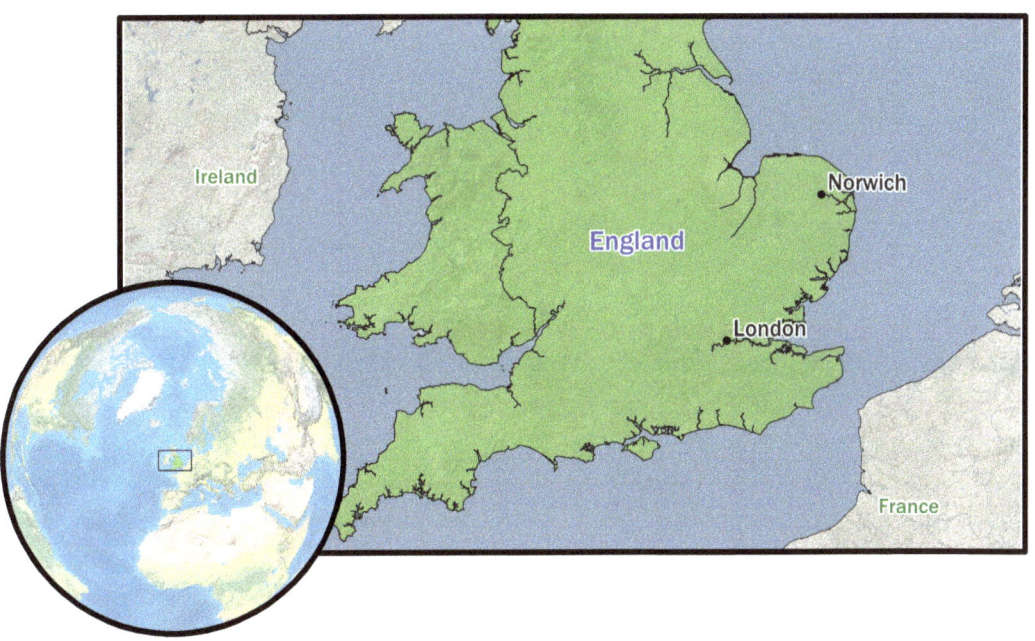

Julian of Norwich is famous for writing the earliest surviving religious text by a woman in England.

Not much is known of Julian's early life, and it is not even known if 'Julian' was her real name. It may be the name of the church that she belonged to. Julian lived in Norwich, England, which was a wealthy city in the 1300s, second only in importance to the capital, London.

In 1373, at the age of thirty, Julian became seriously ill. She was so ill that she thought she was going to die. One night during her illness, **she received visions** of Jesus Christ – fifteen visions, in fact. She then had one more vision the next night. After this, Julian recovered from her illness back to full health, and she saw this as a miracle. She wrote down her visions and spent the rest of her life trying to understand them.

Julian became an *anchoress* in St. Julian's Church of Norwich. It's not known if she was part of the church as a nun or an anchoress before she received her visions, or afterwards. An anchorite or anchoress was a Christian who **chose to live in one small room or place** for the rest of their life, devoting their time to God. Some even had their door walled up so they could not be tempted to leave, with only a window to receive their food through and to talk to visitors.

As an anchoress, living in her small room, **Julian wrote about her visions** and what she believed they meant. Her writings are called *Revelations of Divine Love,* and they are the **earliest surviving works written in English by a woman**, and the only surviving work in English by an anchoress!

Her writings talk about God being all-forgiving, no matter what a person may have done. She said that God loved everyone. **She was known in Norwich and beyond** during her life, and she had many visitors who came and spoke to her through her window, asking for advice, guidance, and prayers. England was very religious during this time, and people came to speak with the devout anchoress, holding her in high regard.

Julian's writings stayed with the church after her death, and they were not copied down until a few hundred years later in 1670. Many centuries later, in 1901, the manuscript was found, recopied and updated (the English language had changed a lot over the centuries, so it had to be updated for people to understand), and published again. *Revelations of Divine Love* is still in print today.

INTERESTING FACTS:

Julian is famous for creating the saying, 'All will be well, and all shall be well, and all manner of things shall be well.'

Although Julian's was the first English written work on religion by a woman, Europe had already enjoyed a golden age of women's religious writing – so there were more writings by women in other languages around at this time.

After Julian died, the cell where she lived was used continuously by others, until the 1530s.

St Julian's Church in Norwich as it may have looked in the middle ages. Julian lived here in a small room for many years, never leaving.

Christine de Pizan

Lived: 1364 C.E. - 1430 C.E.
Location: Italy, France
Occupation: Professional Writer

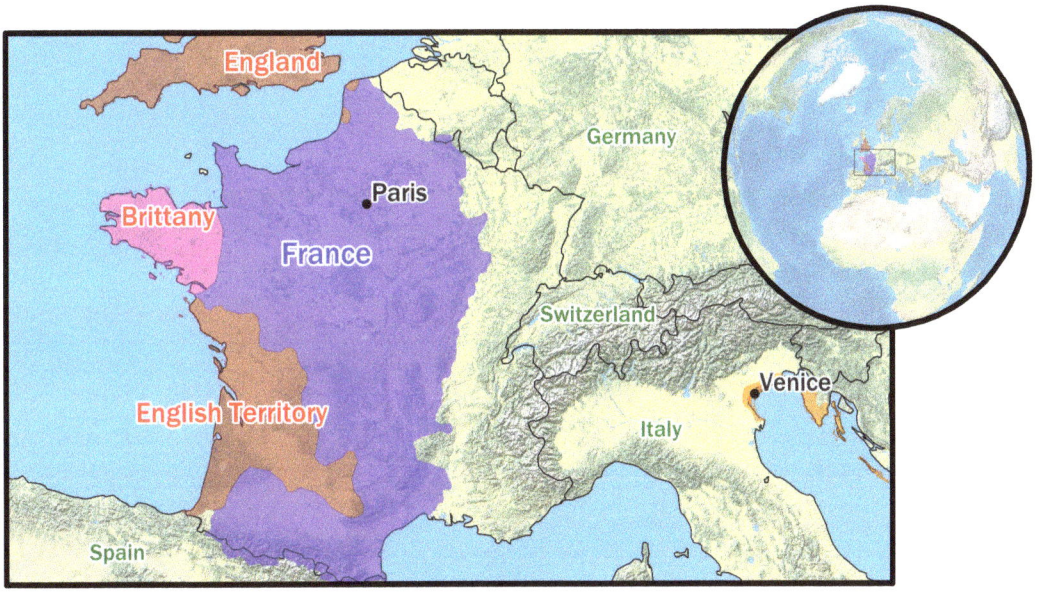

Christine de Pizan was a noble lady who gained fame and reputation through her writing, and who became a favourite of the French royal court. She was the first woman we know of to make her living from writing.

Born in Italy, Christine's father was an important man at the royal court: he was the Italian king's physician and astrologer. He must have been good, because the king of France, *Charles V,* asked him to come and be his astrologer instead! In 1368, when Christine was age three, the Pizan family moved to France and entered into royal life there.

> ### INTERESTING FACT:
> *Astrology was the practice of looking at the position of the stars on someone's birth date to determine good or bad fortune for that person. An astrologer was meant to be able to tell if an action would go well or not by looking at the pattern of stars and planets. Many rulers had personal astrologers during this period in history.*

Christine enjoyed writing, and it was her poetry that first caught the attention of others. However, she was well educated, and so **she also wrote about politics** – a subject not usually discussed by women, as politics and leadership roles were only for men.

Christine married and had three children, but tragedy struck their family when she was just twenty-five years old. Her husband caught the plague and died. Christine had to find a way to support her mother, niece, and children. Although her family had been wealthy, the law courts told her that her husband had owed lots of money, so Christine did not inherit any of her husband's wealth.

To support the family, Christine began writing in earnest. She wrote love ballads, novels, poetry, philosophy, and letters on politics and religion – quite an extensive list for anyone at the time! She became **so successful at writing** that the noblemen of the court – and the princess herself – wanted to read her works.

Christine's writings on every subject were so excellent that rich nobility **actually paid for her to print books** of her writing, so that they could have copies of them. Publishing books was not common at this time, because all books had to be **written by hand** and the pages carefully bound together. It took a lot of skill and a long time, so a person had to be very wealthy indeed to commission a copy of a book.

Not only was she the **first woman we know of to be paid for her writing,** but Christine also personally oversaw the illumination of her books. This was the process of creating beautiful artwork that illustrated some of the letters on each page, and some illustrative pictures, too. Using coloured inks to create beautiful colours in a manuscript was expensive, and it was all done by hand. (And you had to hope that no one would make a mistake, otherwise they would have to start the whole page all over again!)

Christine's fame spread further as she was able to continue writing and producing these books with all the money paid to her. In total, Christine wrote forty-one poems and other written pieces. The queen herself, *Queen Isabeau* of France, even commissioned a book with all of Christine's works in one volume! The book included beautiful illustrations, and there was a **picture on the front cover of Christine with the Queen** – a true mark of success!

Christine was not shy in her writing: against the norms of the time, she was an outspoken **defender of women.** This was something not normally written or even spoken about, as men mainly expected women to stay quiet and to do as they were told! It seems that Christine did not, in fact, 'do as she was told', scolding men in her writing and arguing on political and religious matters with them. She even **wrote a treatise on military warfare** – and despite being written by a woman, this book was popular and well received. Christine was loved by not only the royal court, but by all of Europe for her brilliant writing.

Christine lived a long and, we can assume, happy life, and died at the age of sixty-five or sixty-six, having lived a life of true accomplishment.

INTERESTING FACT:

Christine lived in the time of the 100 Years' War, 1337-1453. France and England were at war and England controlled parts of France. The English king believed he had a claim to the French throne. This period includes the famous battle of Agincourt, which Henry V of England won, with devastating losses to the French. The war was on and off during this time, with many battles, and claims to parts of the French land. Christine indeed lived during a turbulent time of political upheavals.

SAYYIDA AL-HURRA
(Sy-eeda al-hur-ra)

Lived: 1485 C.E. - 1561 C.E.
Location: Morocco
Occupation: Ruler, Pirate

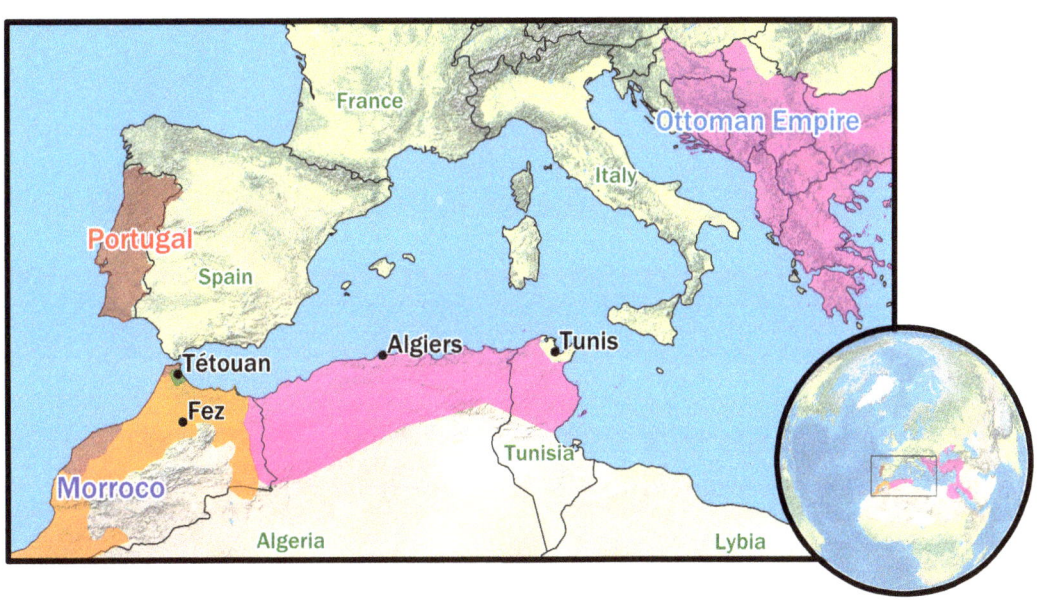

Sayyida al-Hurra is known today as one of the most important women of the Islamic West. Her real name was Lalla Aicha bint Ali ibn Rashid al-Alami. The name Sayyida al-Hurra was actually a title, meaning, 'noble lady who is free and independent'.

alla was born into a noble Muslim family. They had to flee from their home in Spain when Lalla was young, to Morocco in North Africa, because of an ongoing war between Muslims and Christians.

INTERESTING FACT:

From the early 700s up until 1492, Spain or territories within Spain was invaded and controlled at various times by Muslim states. In Lalla's time, the Islamic Emirate of Granada controlled a southern portion of Spain, but in 1492 they were defeated by Spanish Christians and ceded control.

As she grew up, Lalla learnt to speak several languages. She was married at the age of sixteen to an older man – her husband then became the governor of Tetouan in northern Morocco, and **Lalla was entrusted to manage the state** every time he left on business. When he died in 1515, Lalla was **accepted as the governor** by the people and was given the title '*al-Hurra*'.

At the same time as being busy ruling the state, Sayyida al-Hurra was a privateer – **a pirate** who acted under legal protection, with the backing of the state. (Well, who was going to argue with her, seeing as she was the ruling governor?!) She turned to privateering because she wanted to take revenge on the Christians who had invaded her homeland all those years ago and forced her family to flee. She was **incredibly successful at piracy,** and she entered into a partnership with the famous pirate *Barbarossa*. They split the Mediterranean Sea between them, with Barbarossa controlling the eastern side and al-Hurra controlling the west. She took many captives and plenty of treasure, but she was also famed in Spain and beyond for **releasing her captives.**

Al-Hurra ruled from 1515 to 1542, and in 1541 she remarried – this time marrying the sultan (king) of Morocco! **She refused to go to her husband-to-be for the marriage** to take place, instead forcing him to leave his capital of Fez to come to her. Many see this as al-Hurra making a powerful statement that she would not give up her rule for anyone, not even a king! It is the only known incident of a Moroccan king leaving his capital to marry.

A year after her marriage, **al-Hurra was overthrown** by her own son-in-law. He stripped her of her property and power, and she left her state peacefully. Away from the life that she had lived for such a long time, al-Hurra lived for another twenty years.

Governor, pirate, and wife of a sultan, Sayyida al-Hurra led an extraordinary life indeed!

> ### INTERESTING FACT:
> Barbarossa had the nickname 'Redbeard'. He had an incredible career, famously capturing Algeria (in North Africa) from Spain with his brother. They were privateers, authorised to pirate by the Ottoman empire, to raid and defeat any enemy ships. Barbarossa captured many Spanish ships during his time of privateering.

This type of ship is called a **galley**, it had oars and small sails. It was very popular with the early Mediterranean pirates including **Sayyida**.

HWANG JINI
(Hu-ang Jini)

Lived: 1506 C.E. - 1567 C.E.
Location: Korea
Occupation: Poet

Hwang Jini was also known under several other names: Hwang Jin-yi and Myeongwol, which means 'bright moon'.

Hwang Jini lived in Korea. She was the granddaughter of a politician, so her family had a high status in society. However, her mother was a commoner and so had no status. Korea had a strict hierarchy, and because her mother was not from a well-born family, **Hwang Jini was considered an outcast.** She did not have the wealth and privilege of her father's family. Despite this, Jini seems to have had many wonderful qualities: she was charming, quick-witted, beautiful, intelligent, and importantly, independent.

Life for women in Korea during this time was very restrictive, with women expected to remain indoors and perform wifely duties – the laundry, the tidying, and having children. Jini decided that **this was not the life for her,** and she chose to become a courtesan instead. Courtesans, also known as *kisaeng*, were women from low class families who trained in **poetry, music and dance.** Accomplished in these arts, they acted as talented entertainers for wealthy people.

Hwang Jini became famous in her role at court, not only because of her beauty, but because of her wit and her intellect as well. Courtesans often gave their guests a riddle to solve, and **Hwang Jini's riddle became famous** because it was so difficult and clever. It is said that only one man ever solved her riddle.

She also **wrote her own poetry,** and that too has become famous for its beauty and cleverness – indeed, Jini seems a remarkable woman of her time, captivating all around her and mastering all the arts that she was trained in. She wrote poems about her life, which gave the people of the time a glimpse into her world. Her poems still survive today and have been translated into English. They are also still sometimes taught in schools in Korea.

INTERESTING FACT:

Korean script uses symbols, similar to Chinese, and different to the English alphabet. It was the use of these symbols and the way that they could be combined in different ways that Hwang Jini made her riddle. The answer to it was in the riddle itself: by taking two of the symbols and putting them together, they created the answer!

Hwang Jini has a crater named after her on planet Venus.

Grace O'Malley

Lived: 1530 C.E. - 1603 C.E.
Location: Ireland
Occupation: Pirate

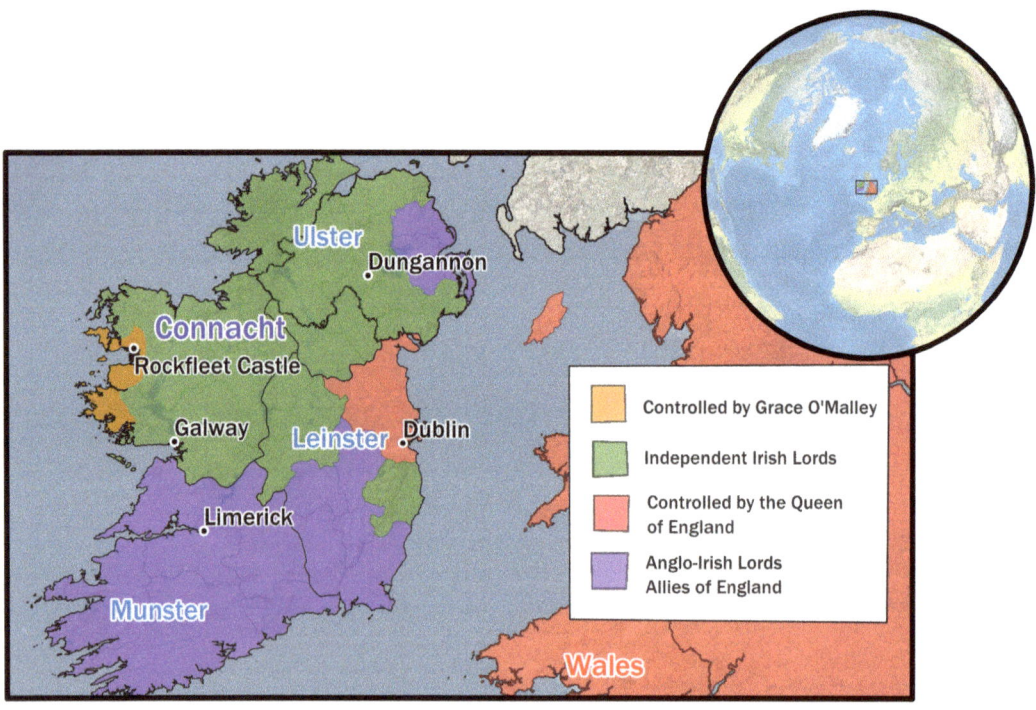

Grace's name in Irish was Grainne Ni Mhaille, but she is known to the world as Grace O'Malley – a leader, a fighter, and fearless.

Grace's father was the chief of a clan based in the west of Ireland. Their family were well to-do – they were a sea faring clan and owned several castles, all of which faced the sea to protect their lands from enemies. The O'Malleys collected taxes from anyone who fished off their coasts. When her father died, **Grace took over leadership** of the family, even though she had an older brother. She was smart and influential, and well-versed in running the household and their lands.

Grace married and had two children, but tragedy struck when her husband was killed in an ambush by a rival branch of his family. These rivals then moved to take Grace's castle, but Grace, no quiet meek woman, fought back and **forced the enemy to withdraw**, saving her castle and her lands.

Sometime later, Grace rescued a shipwrecked sailor and fell in love with him. They only spent a short time together, however, before he too was killed by a rival clan. In revenge, Grace, fearless and tough, **attacked the rival clan at Doona Castle**. She and her 200 men won, capturing the castle. In her honour, the castle was renamed 'Hen's Castle.'

Grace was fierce in protecting her lands and her territory at sea. She and her men roamed as far as Scotland and Spain, raiding ships in acts of piracy. During this time, there was conflict between the English and the Irish. The English held lands in Ireland, which the Irish were resisting. At one point, a force of English soldiers penned Grace and her army in one of her castles. Trapped there for twenty-one days, Grace eventually decided to lead her men out to face their enemy. They charged at the English, who then fled!

Grace later married again, this time to *'Iron Richard' Bourke*. She had a third child and was **on her ship when she gave birth**. The day after her son was born, her ship was attacked by other pirates, and her men called for help. In a rage at their 'uselessness', Grace carefully put her baby down and stomped up on deck, fighting furiously and repelling the invaders!

INTERESTING FACT:

↬Although the Irish were Christian, they held old traditional customs on marriage, and a woman could divorce a man.
↬After a year, Grace, in the castle owned by her husband Richard, locked him out by barring the castle against him with her men, and telling him that she was divorcing him. She kept his castle!

As the conflict with England gathered pace, Grace's son and half-brother were captured by the English magistrate, **accused of rebellion** against England. What happened next was extraordinary: Grace wrote to the queen, the great and famous *Elizabeth I,* and then, in order to secure the release of her family members, **she sailed to England to meet the queen** in person!

Elizabeth I, Queen of England, met with Grace – an Irish noble *and* a pirate! This was an incredible meeting. No-one knows what was said between the two as the meeting was a private one, but Grace must have impressed Queen Elizabeth, because **the queen ordered the release of Grace's family** with goodwill and good wishes.

Grace O'Malley eventually died at the age of about seventy-two. She died in the very same year as Queen Elizabeth I: 1603. Perhaps these two powerful women, from very different backgrounds, found something in common in their experiences: that of being independent women in a world where men usually held all the power. Perhaps the Queen of England saw in Grace a woman of strength and free spirit. We will never know… but it's a nice thing to think!

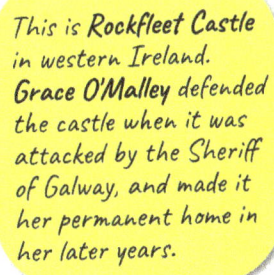

This is **Rockfleet Castle** in western Ireland. **Grace O'Malley** defended the castle when it was attacked by the Sheriff of Galway, and made it her permanent home in her later years.

Amina of Zazzau

Lived: 1533 C.E. - 1610 C.E.
Location: Zazzau, Nigeria
Occupation: Warrior Queen

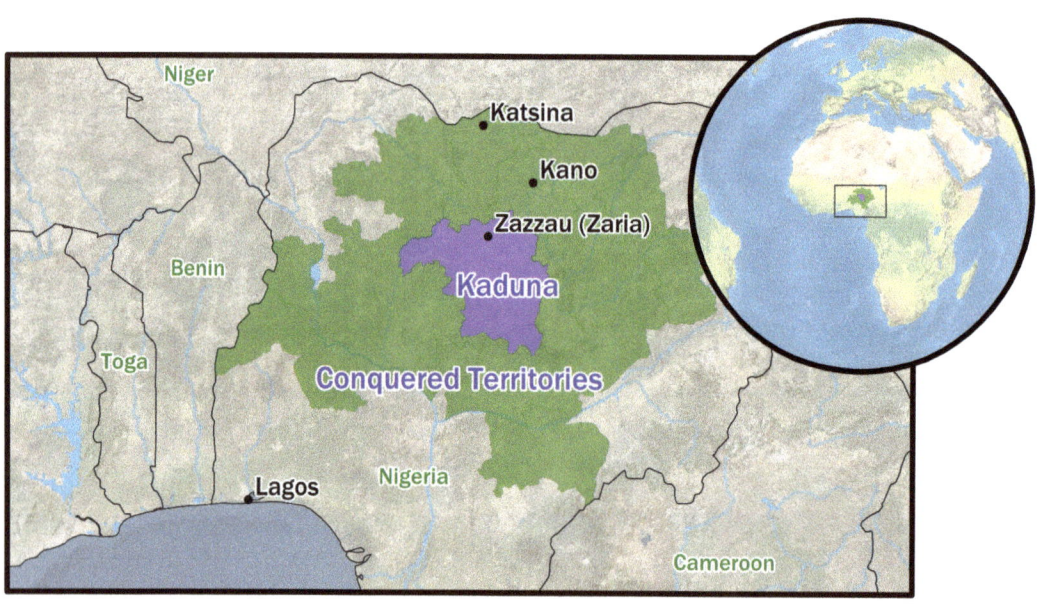

Amina of Zazzau (now known as Zaria in Nigeria) was the daughter of the king. She became queen, and is known for being an excellent military strategist.

Amina grew up as a princess, and a favourite of her grandfather, who made sure that she was **well educated in politics**. Amina's father was the king, and when he died, her brother became king instead. Amina had been trained in war tactics by her grandfather and **joined the cavalry** under her brother's leadership, quickly making a reputation for herself as a superb warrior.

When her brother, *Karami*, died in 1576, Amina became the queen. Only a few months after taking the throne, she declared war on the surrounding states. She wanted to expand the territory of her country, Zazzau. Calling on her people, Amina gathered an army of thousands She waged a **thirty-four-year campaign** to conquer neighbouring areas and bringing them under her rule (that's a *very* long campaign!). She must have been superbly confident in her own might and power, as well as her military skills. Everywhere she went, Amina won battles. Once she had taken over a place, she had **earthen walls** built around the town to surround and protect it. This meant that it would be much harder for another army to take the town for their own, as they would have to break through the walls first. The walls that Amina built around each town lasted from her time right up until 1904! That's **300 years!** Some of them still survive today.

From far and wide, Amina was given goods and money as a tribute by the places that she conquered. This made her wealthy, and it meant that she could continue with her campaign to grow her territories. A tribute was a way for towns and villages to show their loyalty to their new ruler.

As well as successfully expanding her territory and protecting it against any enemy who might try to attack and gain control, Amina also **created trade routes** throughout northern Africa. This meant that goods from one place could get more easily to others. This increased trade, and created wealth for the merchants who sold the goods and each of the towns that traded. So everyone was happy about this! Amina's successes are still remembered today in traditional Hausa songs – for example, one that features the lyrics: *"Amina daughter of Nikatau, a woman as capable as a man that was able to lead men..."*

INTERESTING FACT
There is a statue to Queen Amina in Lagos state, and there are many institutions today that are named after her.

NUR JAHAN
(Nur Ja-han)

Lived: 1577 C.E. - 1645 C.E.
Location: Lahore, India
Occupation: Empress

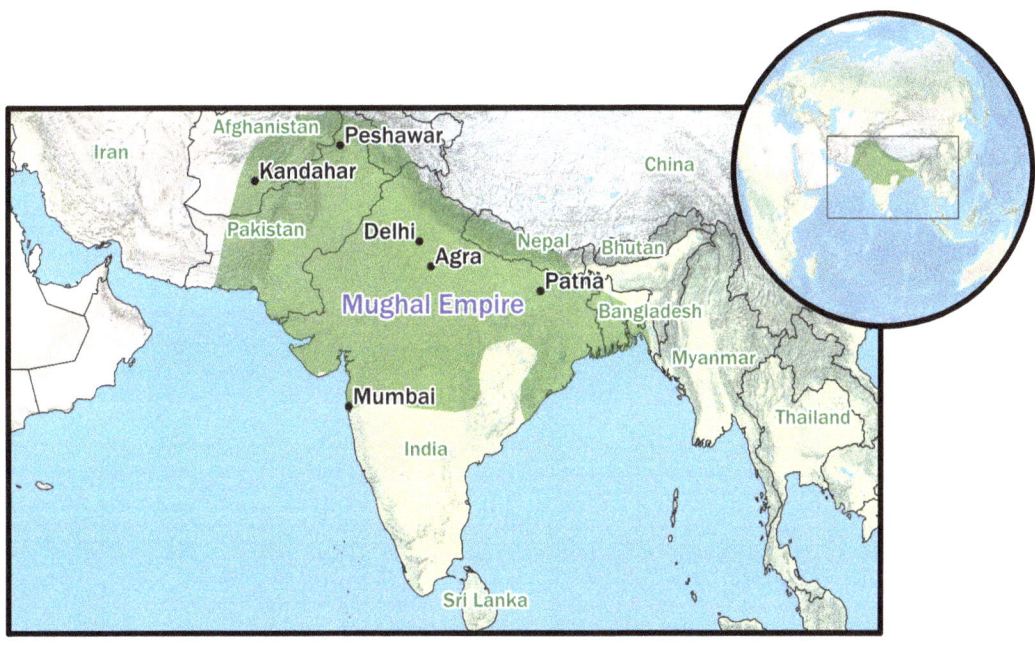

Nur Jahan's real name was Mehr-Un-Nissa, which means 'sun among women'. She was given the name Nur Jahan when she married the emperor of the Mughal Empire in India.

Nur Jahan came from a noble and wealthy family who lived in Persia. Wealthy, that was, until they fell on hard times and had to leave their home. Travelling to India, Nur Jahan's father was lucky enough to meet a friend who arranged a job for him in the emperor's court. The family were once again able to prosper.

At the age of seventeen, Nur Jahan married, and she had a daughter a few years later. Sadly, her husband died when their daughter was very young. Nur Jahan travelled back to court to live at the royal palace where her father worked. **The emperor, on seeing her, fell in love.** They were soon married, and she was given the name Nur Jahan, which means 'light of the world'. Her husband, the emperor, trusted her so much that **he gave her the royal seal.** This meant that she had the final say on decrees and decisions! She had a lot of political power, and as her husband loved to go hunting a lot, she made many decisions for the whole empire. It was incredibly rare for a woman of the Mughal Empire to be given this much power and influence.

In 1626, enemy rebels captured the emperor. Nur Jahan was not content to rely on others getting him back, so **she rode out herself at the head of a small army,** riding a war elephant! She also commanded the army, organising the rescue mission. The rebels fought against them, and Nur Jahan's elephant was hit. The rebels then captured her as well. But Nur Jahan did not give up – she was not going to stay meekly as a prisoner! She hatched a plan, and managed to **free herself and the emperor** as well, escaping from their captors.

Not only was Nur Jahan clever in politics, and brave in fighting, but she also gave lots of money to have beautiful buildings designed and built, including gardens and palaces. She also made contributions to all kinds of art, and the creation of textiles for clothes.

INTERESTING FACTS:

It was common for Mughal women of nobility and wealth to commission buildings and gardens, and to share their wealth with arts or education,.

This era also saw women act as bodyguards to the women of the royal court. The tradition of female bodyguards started in 300 B.C.E, under the rule of Chandragupta Maurya, the founder of the Indian Mauryan Empire.

Njinga
(N-jin-ga)

Lived: 1583 C.E. - 1663 C.E.
Location: Ndongo, Africa
Occupation: Warrior Queen

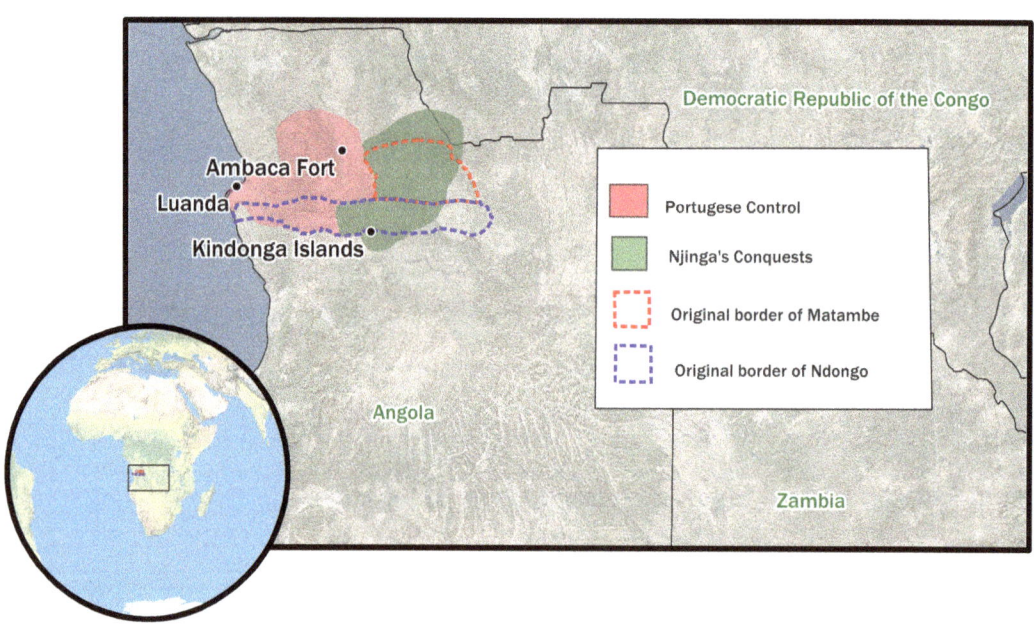

Njinga was a princess of the royal family in Ndongo, known today as Angola, in central west Africa. She is still remembered for being a fierce, uncompromising leader of her people.

Njinga's father was the king. He had a lot of troubles, because he had to protect his kingdom against its neighbours, who were bandits and raiders, and also from Europeans who were sailing to Africa to take slaves. He raised his daughter Njinga to fight as well as to understand politics, and she became an excellent warrior.

Njinga's brother became king after their father died. He was trying to protect his kingdom from the Portuguese, who were taking land and people. He knew that Njinga was very clever, and as Njinga spoke Portuguese, he asked her to **negotiate a peace treaty**. Njinga went with many servants and dressed in full royal clothing, to show that this was a meeting of equals. She wanted the Europeans to know that she was acting on behalf of the king. Arriving in the hall, she saw that there was no chair out for her to sit on. The Portuguese wanted to make her uncomfortable so that they would have an advantage in the talks. But Njinga simply waved a hand, and one of her servants immediately knelt down in front of her, on their hands and knees. **Njinga sat on the back of the servant,** using them as a chair. This put her at the same height as the Portuguese governor, who was most put out by this display of power.

Njinga was very adept in her talks with the Portuguese governor. She was successful, bringing back to her brother a peace treaty between their nations. Her people clapped and cheered, celebrating her success. However, the treaty did not last long, and Ndongo found itself in battles with the Portuguese who once again wanted to take over the land.

When Njinga's brother died in 1624, having been defeated many times, Njinga became *Ngola* - the ruler. She was determined to change Ndongo's fortunes and to remove the Portuguese from their lands. She knew that she could not fight head on because the Portuguese were better armed, so she tried to talk with them again. But the Portuguese would **not recognise her** as a legitimate ruler, because she was female, and so they would not accept her demands. Two years later, the Portuguese **declared war** on Ndongo. Although Njinga raised an army and fought them, eventually her forces were overwhelmed and she had to flee into exile. Not one to give up, though, Njinga married a war chief named *Kasanje* and used his warriors to rebuild her army. Njinga was able to **disrupt the trade routes** of the Portuguese across her kingdom, which stopped them from being able to take slaves. She fought with her men in the battles herself, being a trained and fierce warrior. All this disruption to their trade greatly angered the Portuguese, and they were determined to get rid of Njinga for good.

Njinga spent several years capturing the neighbouring kingdom of Matamba, giving her a powerful base from which to continue fighting. Then she made another political move. In 1641, Njinga entered an **alliance with the Dutch**, who were competing with the Portuguese for land and slaves. Njinga did this because she thought of the saying, 'the enemy of my enemy is my friend'. She thought that the Dutch could help her get rid of the Portuguese once and for all.

With the help of her new allies, Njinga was able to **reclaim much of her Ndongo lands.** However, the Portuguese fought back and eventually won against the Dutch, who then left Ndongo. This meant Njinga was once again fighting her enemy alone. With political talks and fierce fighting continuing for **twenty-five years,** both sides were eventually exhausted. Finally, a peace treaty was agreed and signed in 1656, with both Njinga and the Portuguese recognising the rights of each other and making compromises. Twenty-five years is a long time for a war – and Njinga **held on to her power** for all that time. She may have had to flee to exile, start again more than once, having lost warriors and some of her land – but she always came back, fighting, determined, and continuing to face her enemy. By the time of the treaty of 1656, she was old, having only taken the throne at the age of thirty-five. She fell ill in 1663 and died at the age of eighty years old.

Njinga forged a powerful legacy, and today she is still remembered in her native Angola (the modern name for her homeland of Ndongo) and beyond. She is even known by many as 'the mother of Angola.'

INTERESTING FACTS:

Njinga often wore men's clothes. Her rule was resisted by some nobles in Ndongo because she was a woman. She became known as 'the female king'. She was fighting a political war with her own people, as well as her battles with the Portuguese.

Njinga made her sister, Kambu, her successor. For 100 years after Njinga's death, women ruled for eighty of those years!

Jahanara Begum
(Ja-han-ara Bay-gum)

Lived: 1614 C.E. - 1681 C.E.
Location: India
Occupation: Princess

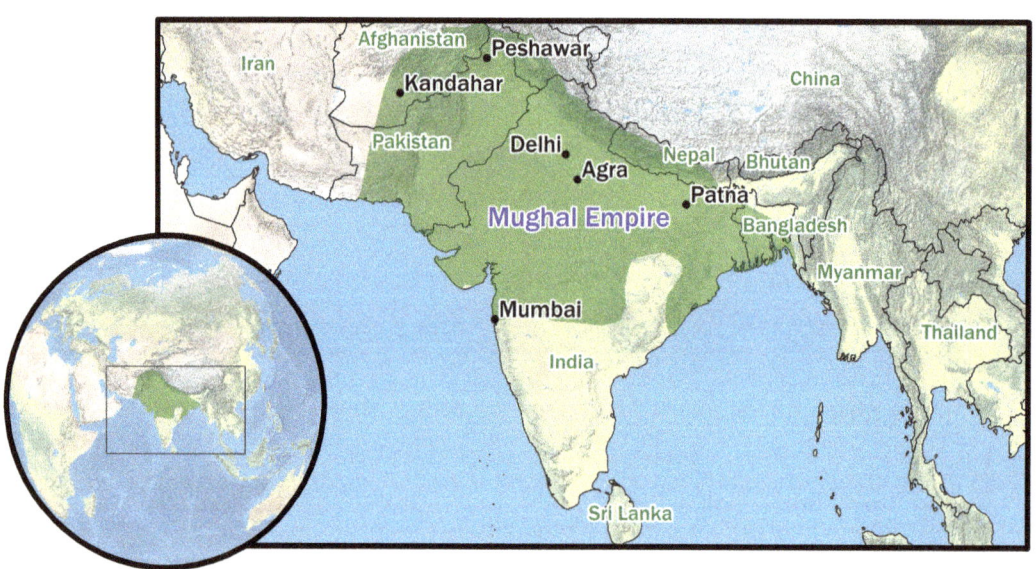

Jahanara Begum was the niece of Nur Jahan (see page 130) and she was just as impressive as her aunt. Born into luxurious wealth and privilege, the princess did not rest meekly in luxury – she has a place in history because of her attitude, her clever mind, and what she achieved.

Princess Jahanara was well versed in politics and diplomacy by the time she was a teenager. Her father, *Shah Jahan*, ruled the *Mughal Empire*, and she became her father's **close adviser and confidante** – not a position usually given to a woman.

Jahanara had her own wealth, and she **owned her own ship and port**. She gave often and generously to the poor, making donations and sending food to the people. She also used her money to help fund learning and the arts. Devoutly spiritual in the *Sufi* religion, Jahanara also made such good progress in this regard that she would have been named as **successor of a Sufi leader,** but sadly the rules did not allow women to do so.

> ### INTERESTING FACTS:
>
> The Mughal Empire was an area that covered most of India except the south, plus Bangladesh and Pakistan. The Mughal Empire lasted for just over 300 years, from 1526 to 1857.
>
> Sufism is a religious practice within Islam.
>
> Jahanara's father was Shah Jahan, and her mother was Mumtaz Mahal. Mumtaz was loved so much by her husband that he built the famous Taj Mahal in her honour after she died.
>
> Mumtaz Mahal had political power herself. She held the emperor's seal, which meant nothing could be done without her consent. Mumtaz also gave donations to the poor and ordered the building of a famous riverside garden.

Jahanara organised the **design of a great market place,** known as the *Chandni Chowk*. This was a **whole market full of shops** with a great pool in the centre, designed to reflect the moonlight. She also paid for a mosque to be built. As well as all this, she also found time to write several books!

The princess had thirteen siblings (a LOT of brothers and sisters!). Two of her brothers hated each other so much that they actually went to war, fighting against one another. When one of the brothers won, he imprisoned his father for taking the other brother's side, and then took the throne. Jahanara **chose to follow her father into prison** rather than remain in her luxury and wealth. She stayed with him and cared for him for eight years, until he died. After his death, her brother freed her, **restored her status**, and gave her back all her wealth.

Jahanara was not just a princess: she used her political influence, gave to the poor, followed a spiritual path, wrote books, and ordered great buildings made. She was indeed a great princess, woman, and human being.

> ### INTERESTING FACT:
>
> There were other notable Mughal women:
>
> Gulbadan Begum (1523-1603) was the daughter of Emperor Babur, the founder of the Mughal Empire. She wrote about her father's life, and that the royal court was nomadic, living in encampments rather than staying in palaces.
>
> Roshanara Begum (1617-1671) Sister of Jahanara, she was a poet. She foiled a plot to kill her brother, Aurangzeb. He gave her the royal seal as thanks. But she was eventually stripped of this power when the emperor found out that she was greedy and corrupt. She is known for the building of the Roshanara Garden.
>
> Zeb-Un-Nissa, (1638-1702). Daughter of Aurangzeb, and niece of Jahanara. She was a poet who had her works published under the title 'The Complete Works of Makhfi.' She apparently memorised the Ko'ran in three years, earning the title of 'Hafiza'.
>
> Jahanzeb Banu Begum (birth date unknown - 1705). Known as 'Jani', she was niece to Jahanara. She was looked after by her aunt Roshanara, as both her parents had died. Her aunt treated her badly. Jani was sent to the prison where Shah Jahan and Jahanara were, and there she was taught and educated by Jahanara. She was later freed from the prison.

Anne Bonny

Lived: Unknown date of birth - 1720 C.E. or later
Location: Ireland, the Caribbean
Occupation: Pirate

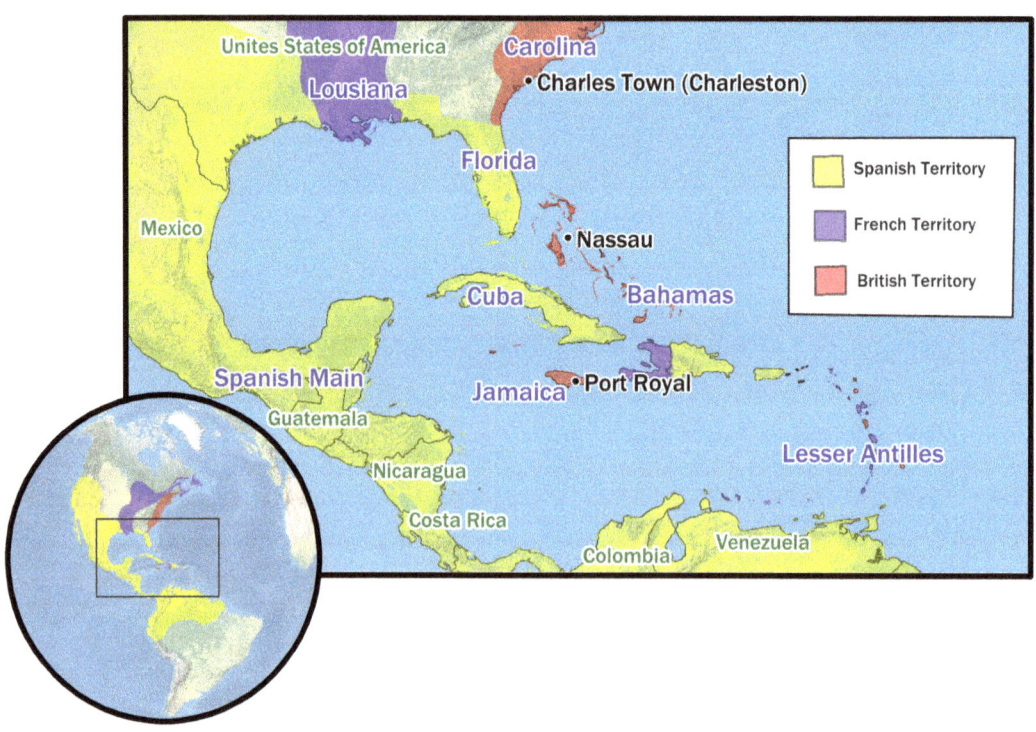

About 100 years after Grace O'Malley, another Irish woman took to the pirate life – her name was Anne Bonny.

Born as Anne Cormac, Anne Bonny's father was a lord and her mother a servant woman. They lived in County Cork, Ireland. When Anne was ten years old, the family moved from Ireland to the province of Carolina in America, which was under English rule. Anne was **dressed as a boy** by her father, so that she could serve as his assistant in his work.

> ### INTERESTING FACT:
>
> During this time period, America was not the 'United States' that we know today, but was settled by different European and religious communities across the many different areas. For example, the Carolinas were owned by Britain; Alabama and Mississippi were Spanish; Louisiana was French. There was a lot of competition for the land. The American War of Independence, when the British colonies in America fought to gain its independence from England was in 1775 – just thirty years after Anne Bonny.

Some years later, when she was grown, Anne married *James Bonny*. Her father did not approve of this man, and he disowned her. She and her husband left, moving to the Caribbean Island of Nassau, a place known as a **sanctuary for pirates.** Anne visited the taverns (pubs) of Nassau, mingling with the pirates there. She met *Jack Rackham* – also known as 'Calico Jack' – and ran away with him, becoming a **member of his pirate crew**. She later divorced James and married Rackham.

As women were extremely rare as pirates, Anne **disguised herself as a man** – just as her friend *Mary Read* did, who was another well-known female pirate. They may have only disguised themselves as men when they engaged another ship. Ship life was cramped and restricted with barely any personal space, so it would have been difficult for women to keep up the pretence of being men with their own crew.

Bonny, Read, and Rackham **sailed the Caribbean seas** with their pirate crew, and the two women **took part in battles** alongside the men, frequently raiding merchant vessels. The women wore long trousers and men's jackets, each holding a pistol and a sword.

INTERESTING FACT:

Jack Rackham is said to have flown and possibly even designed his own version of the most famous pirate flag, The Jolly Roger. However, there is no real evidence of this and he was known to have flown a white pendant flag.

It used to be thought that Calico Jack flew the 'Jolly Roger' but the only record says he flew a <u>white triangular</u> 'Pendant'

Pirates raided merchant vessels from any and every country, taking what goods they could to sell and make themselves rich. This **disrupted trade routes,** and the British and Americans – as well as the Dutch and Portuguese, who sailed the coasts of America – were desperate to stop the pirates. They sent out their own ships, more heavily armed with guns and cannons than merchant ships were, to try and capture the pirates.

The crew were **eventually caught** in 1720. The men had been drinking the night before and were not in a fit state to fight. Anne scolded Rackham, saying,:

"*Had you fought like a man, you would not now hang.*"
They were all taken away and imprisoned.

There is no record of Anne Bonny's death. It is thought that she may have been released from prison and returned to America. What became of her after this remains a mystery.

MARY READ

Lived: 1685 C.E. - 1721 C.E.
Location: England, the Caribbean
Occupation: Pirate

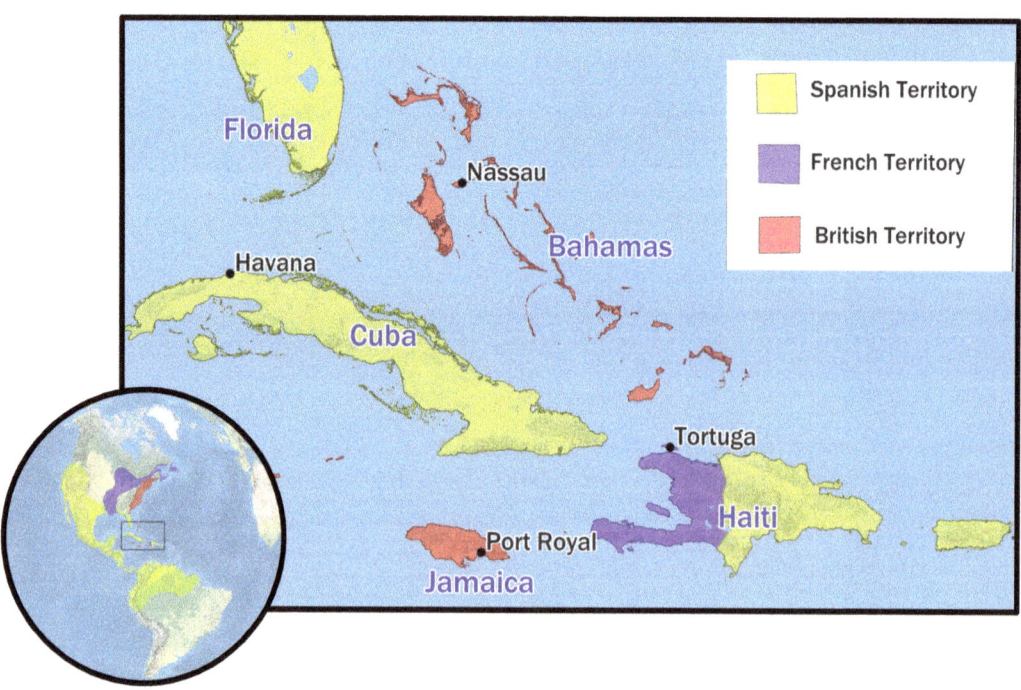

Mary Read was another female pirate, and she sailed with Calico Jack and Anne Bonny.

Mary, like her friend Anne, had an interesting life right from the start: she dressed as a boy from a young age at her mother's insistence. This was so she could get an inheritance from her father's family. Her father had disappeared at sea some time before, and so Mary's mother had no means to support them. Getting money from Mary's grandmother gave them an income to get by.

As a teenager, Mary continued to dress as a boy. **She joined the military** and fought in Flanders in the Netherlands, against the French. She got away with her disguise and earned a **reputation for bravery** fighting in battles.

Later, Mary fell in love with a man who was a fellow soldier, and she admitted her disguise to him. They left the army, got married, and bought an inn where they settled down to live together. Sadly, her husband soon died, and Mary decided to set sail on a ship to the West Indies. **Pirates captured her ship**, and she was taken prisoner. But the pirates who captured her took the king's pardon, which was an amnesty for pirates. It promised that anyone who gave up piracy would not be punished and could live a normal life. This left Mary all alone in a strange place, and this was when she met the pirate *Calico Jack* and decided to join his crew.

Mary and Anne Bonny soon discovered each other's secret – that they were both women – and became good friends. **Mary joined in with raiding** and battles alongside Jack and Anne. Mary, along with Anne Bonny, earned a fierce reputation as that most rare of creatures: **a woman pirate**. After all, at this time, women were meant to be polite, humble, and remain in the home as dutiful wives and mothers!

Mary was captured along with her crew in 1720, and she was imprisoned, where she died from illness in the year 1721. But her independent and unusual life has earned her a place in the history books.

INTERESTING FACT:

In 1724, a book was published, called 'A General History of the Pyrates' by Captain Charles Johnson. It was incredibly popular, giving an exotic telling of the life and times of pirates.

Ng Mui
(Eng Mwee)

Lived: 1700s, C.E.
Location: China
Occupation: Martial Artist

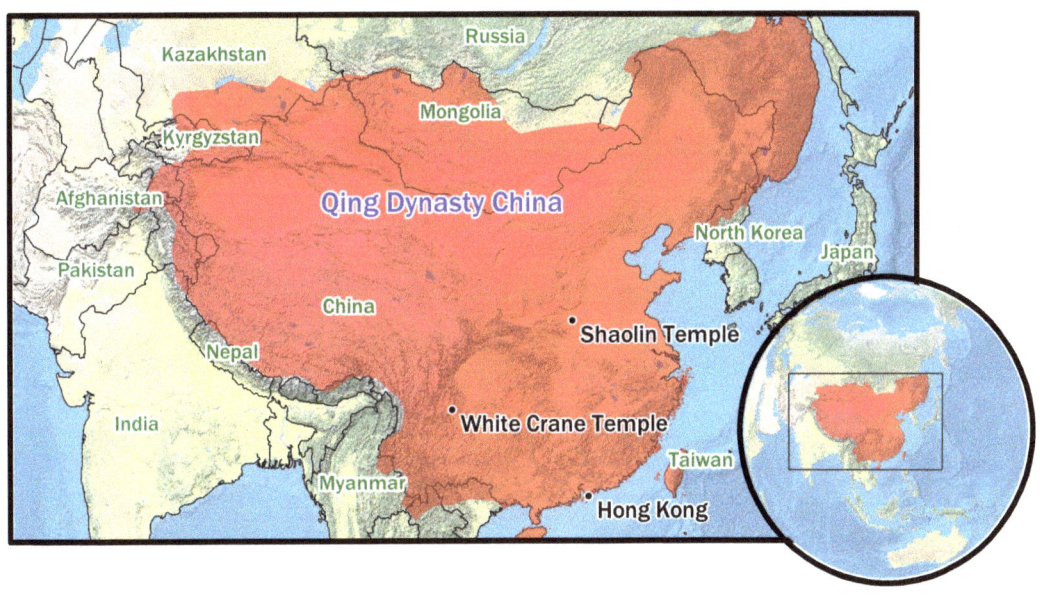

Ng Mui is a mysterious and semi-legendary figure, whose exact origins and early life are unknown. She is said to have lived sometime in the 1700s, although some sources say she lived even earlier.

Ng Mui is known in legends as one of the '*Five Elders*' who survived the destruction of a Shaolin temple. The Five Elders were respected leaders and accomplished martial artists. The Shaolin temple, which was the home of Buddhist monks, was destroyed by the government because it was believed to be helping rebels who were plotting against the ruling state.

Ng Mui fled the temple and went to live elsewhere. Some stories say she then lived at White Crane Temple, carrying her knowledge of martial arts with her. Ng Mui was **already skilled in kung fu**, and she developed several different martial art styles of her own.

> ### INTERESTING FACT:
> *'Kung fu' is a term that covers many different styles of martial arts. Martial art is the practice of fighting and defending oneself using quick precise movements of the whole body, arms and legs. The movements used change depending on the type of style practised.*

Kung fu had been around in China for centuries before Ng Mui. Some believe it goes back to the very first Chinese emperor, thousands of years ago. Over time, **many styles were formed,** by people living in different areas and with different influences. Some styles of kung fu are based on the movements of animals. **Monks and nuns in Shaolin monasteries** practised kung fu, which was both a fighting style and a way to develop the mind, body, and inner energy, known as *chi* or *qi* in China. This focus of energy was very important for monks and nuns.

One day, Ng Mui met a young woman named *Wing Chun* – she was being bothered by a bandit (or it may have been a warlord) who was trying to force her into marriage. Ng Mui took her knowledge of martial arts and **created a new style.** She simplified the techniques so that they could be learnt quickly and did not rely on strength to overcome the enemy. She taught this new style to the young woman, so that she could defend herself against future attacks.

It is from this young woman that the name of Ng Mui's new kung fu comes from: *Wing Chun.* Wing Chun eventually married (a nice man, not a warlord or a bandit!) and she passed her teachings on to her husband. After she died, he taught other people the martial art, and it has **continued all the way down to today,** with people still learning the art of Wing Chun.

This is the **Shanmen (Mountain Gate)** of the **Shaolin Monastery** in Henan Province in China. It is the main entrance to monastery and was rebuilt around the time of **Ng Mui.**

INTERESTING FACT:

In the 1940s, a martial arts expert named Ip Man was living in Hong Kong and teaching a school of Wing Chun. His most famous student was Bruce Lee, who later moved to America and made a lot of famous martial arts movies. It is because of these two figures that Wing Chun spread across the globe and became the most popular kung fu style in the west today.

ZHENG YI SAO

(Jong Yee Sow)

Lived: 1775 C.E. - 1844 C.E.
Location: China
Occupation: Pirate

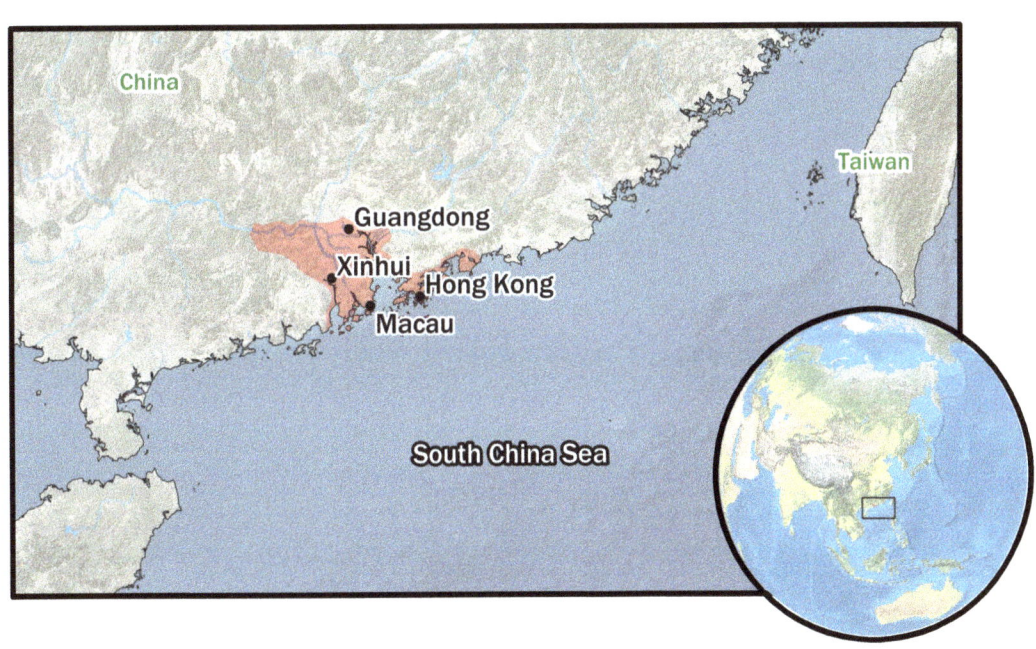

Zheng Yi Sao, also known as Shi Yang and Ching Shih, was a famous Chinese pirate, sailing the South China seas.

Born with the name Shi Yang, this heroine only became Zheng Yi Sao when she married a pirate, *Zheng Yi*. When he died, she took command of his fleet, which was **hundreds of ships and around 40,000 pirates** or more! Zheng Yi Sao is considered one of the most successful pirates **ever**.

Pirates were often in conflict with the authorities, who tried to capture them to stop them from raiding their own vessels and trade ships. Zheng Yi Sao was no different and fought battles **against the powerful East India Company,** the Portuguese, and the government of China. She was a successful pirate for many years.

The pirates that Zheng Yi Sao led were a confederation – other pirate leaders commanding their own fleets agreed to act under the rule first of Zheng Yi, and then after his death, they followed his wife, Zheng Yi Sao. They agreed to give her a percentage of their plunder and coins. **She personally commanded the Black Flag Fleet**, and her husband's adopted son, *Zhang Bao*, commanded the Red Flag Fleet. He did everything he was told to by Zheng Yi Sao.

Zheng Yi Sao personally led several ambushes and battle commands, wiping out enemy ships. The large pirate fleet patrolled the coastline of South China and the riverways, causing real problems to the trade routes. Within a year of Zheng Yi Sao's leadership, they had wiped out sixty-three ships out of a fleet of 135! The Chinese government were desperate to stop them. They asked for help from other countries, who agreed to send ships to go against the pirates, as the piracy was affecting all of their trade. But **Zheng Yi Sao's fleet was so large** and contained so many pirates and ships that the authorities from different countries still could not stop the pirate fleet.

The Chinese government decided that the only thing to do was to **offer the pirates amnesty.** This meant that anyone sailing under the pirate flag was given a pardon for their crimes, and allowed to live freely if they gave up pirating. Zheng Yi Sao knew that this was a good deal, as she understood that she and her men would not be able to be pirates forever. She went to meet the officials to negotiate a deal. In the end, Zheng Yi Sao and her people were **not only pardoned for their crimes** by the state, but they were also allowed to keep all of their goods and money!

Zheng Yi Sao retired from her piracy, along with many others who followed her, and she lived a long life. She died in 1844 at the age of sixty-nine. This is a very happy ending, particularly for a pirate. Zheng Yi Sao lived free, independent, and wealthy... a charmed and lucky life indeed!

INTERESTING FACTS:

Zheng Yi Sao commanded around 400 junks and had between 40,000 and 70,000 pirates at her command!

A 'junk' was a Chinese sailing ship, that sometimes had red sails.

Many people at this time in China lived on boats, on the many rivers and waterways, as it was a good way to make a living for those that were poor. Some families never even stepped foot on land! Because the rivers were vital to people's work and trade, this made piracy very profitable.

.

This ship is a Junk it is a traditional Chinese vessel. Zheng Yi Sao commanded a pirate fleet of 400 of these ships!

WANG CONG'ER

Lived: 1775 C.E. - 1797 C.E.
Location: China
Occupation: Warrior

Wang Cong'er was no noble or princess – she was an ordinary, humble peasant living in China.

Life was tough for the poor in China in the 1700s. Wang's father died when she was young, and so she and her mother had to find money any way they could. They took in other people's laundry to clean, and even took to begging. As a young lady, Wang joined a group of performers, and with them **she learned acrobatics and martial arts,** becoming proficient at kung fu.

As a young woman, Wang met a man named *Qi Ling*. He belonged to a group called the *White Lotus Society.* This group taught the religion of Buddhism, but they were also a **secret anti-government society,** and plotted to bring down the ruling Chinese dynasty. Many believed that the rulers were responsible for the terrible living conditions of poor people. Wang decided to join them, and she married Qi Ling.

The White Lotus Society was made up mainly of peasants, and **many of these were women**. They numbered in the thousands. They were like an army, only smaller and not as well armed as their enemy, the Chinese state army. Therefore, they had to be incredibly careful with how and when they conducted their raids and battles.

Shortly after their marriage, Qi Ling died while fighting. Wang took over leadership of the army, **personally leading 20,000 troops**. She led lightning raids against their enemy – striking suddenly, attacking, and then retreating fast – so that they could not be caught. Wang was victorious, winning battle after battle. Her army joined up with other rebel forces, at its height creating an army numbering over 100,000.

The government army marched to fight Wang and her soldiers head on. Despite being the much smaller group, Wang's people held off the bigger army. They continued to fight unbeaten for over a year with their tenacity, courage, and guerrilla warfare, all under Wang's strategic leadership. At only twenty-two years old, Wang was loved by her army, because she **always attempted to rescue captured soldiers** and she cared for the wounded.

Eventually, though, the White Lotus rebellion was brought to a halt and defeated. Wang Cong'er's legend lived on and inspired further uprisings. These later rebellions eventually brought down the ruling government. Wang Cong'er became a folk hero for the common people of China.

INTERESTING FACT:

The White Lotus Rebellion continued on after Wang Conger's death, until 1804. The Rebellion had started as a protest against unfair taxes that common folk could not afford or pay. The movement gained sympathy among the commoners, and swelled their numbers. Despite being poorly trained, they won against the authorities time and time again, because they used guerilla tactics – lightning raids, instead of head on battles.

This is **Wang Nangxian**, she was another Chinese rebel leader of a different uprising at the same time as **Wang Cong'er**.
She led her people known as the **Bouyei** to fight against the government in south west China. She was defeated and died in 1798 aged just 20.

Lozen

Lived: 1840 C.E. - 1889 C.E.
Location: Arizona, USA
Occupation: Prophet, Seer, Warrior

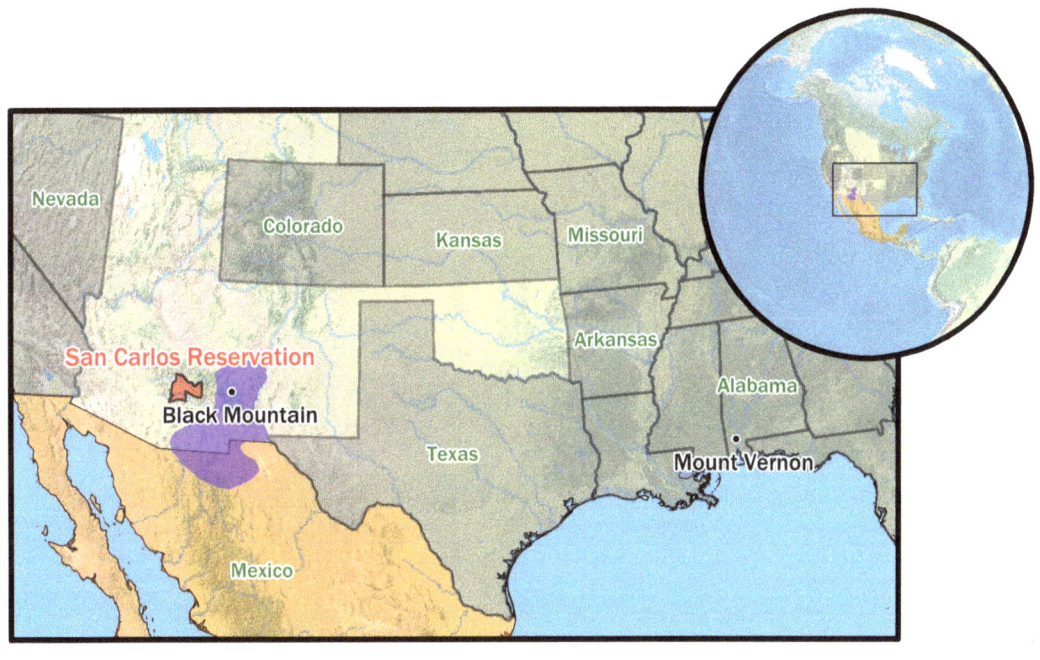

Lozen was an Apache – a native American, or of the First Nation peoples. The Indigenous tribes of America were many and varied, with each tribe having their own customs and beliefs. The Apache lived around the south and south-west of America.

Lozen was the sister of the tribal chief, *Victorio*. Very little is known about her, but 'Lozen' was not her true name; it was a title, meaning 'one who steals horses'. So, she must have been very skilled at stealing enemy horses! She was a **fierce warrior and a great strategist** – so much so that her brother Victorio once introduced her to someone saying: *"Lozen is my right hand… strong as a man, braver than most, and cunning in strategy. Lozen is a shield to her people."*

The First Nation tribes were often in conflict with the European settlers (white Americans), because as more Europeans settled in America and built towns, they were taking the land that the First Nation people already knew as theirs. Many tribes were nomadic, moving from place to place. The new settlers wanted to build and do what they wanted on the land, and so the two groups came into conflict. They had different customs and beliefs, too, which added to the problem.

Lozen became famous for aiding her people in their battles against their enemies. She was always with her brother and his warriors, fighting alongside them. She was not only a warrior, though – which was incredibly rare for a woman – but also **a seer and a prophet**. This was someone who felt they could connect with their god and receive visions or knowledge that no-one else knew. As a seer, Lozen would climb to a high place and stand with her arms outstretched, praying to Ussen, her god. At the end of her prayer, **Lozen would tell her tribe which direction the enemy was coming from.** She would simply *know* where the enemy was. Her people would then move in the opposite direction and evade the enemy, or they would set up an ambush to jump out and surprise them. Lozen was successful with this method time and time again.

On one occasion, Lozen left the warriors to escort a mother and her new-born baby to a place of safety, away from the raiding and the war they were fighting. On their own, they travelled for many days through enemy territory. Not only did Lozen evade capture, but she managed to **creep up on an enemy camp**, and without anyone seeing her, steal some horses and all their gear. They arrived safely at an Apache reservation (where others of her tribe of people lived), where she left the mother and her baby. Lozen then rode for days to return to her warriors and the fighting, again evading capture.

Another time, Lozen led women and children across a raging torrent of a river. The current was so fierce that the women refused to cross, fearing that they would be swept away with the fast-moving water. **Lozen fearlessly walked**

her horse into the river, stopping in the middle of it and holding her rifle high, so that all could see her. Her leadership and courage inspired the women to follow her, and Lozen got all the women and children safely across to the other side.

When her brother Victorio died in battle, Lozen joined forces with another group of Apache warriors, including *Geronimo,* who became famous as a fierce warrior and a shaman (a seer, just like Lozen). She fought by his side, continuing to harry their enemies. Eventually, both were captured and imprisoned.

Lozen's story may end in her confinement, but the tale of her bravery and courage survives to be told to this day.

INTERESTING FACTS:

Not much is known about Lozen, because the First Nation people did not write anything down; they told their stories orally, passing them on by telling them to their children. So, there are no written facts about Lozen's life. As Lozen was special to the Apache because of her role as a seer, they were especially keen to protect her from their enemies.

There were many, many tribes of the First Nation people, and there were different groups of the Apache - Lozen was a Chihenne Chiricahua Apache.

The native people of America, the First Nation people, were persuaded or forced to live on reservations by the white settlers. These reservations were small portions of land compared to where they were used to roaming, and some were forced to move to areas far away from their homeland. This movement in the 1830s-1850s, which caused illness and famine, is known as 'The Trail of Tears.'

NAKANO TAKEKO
(Nak-a-no Tak-ek-o)

Lived: 1847 C.E. - 1868 C.E.
Location: Japan
Occupation: Samurai

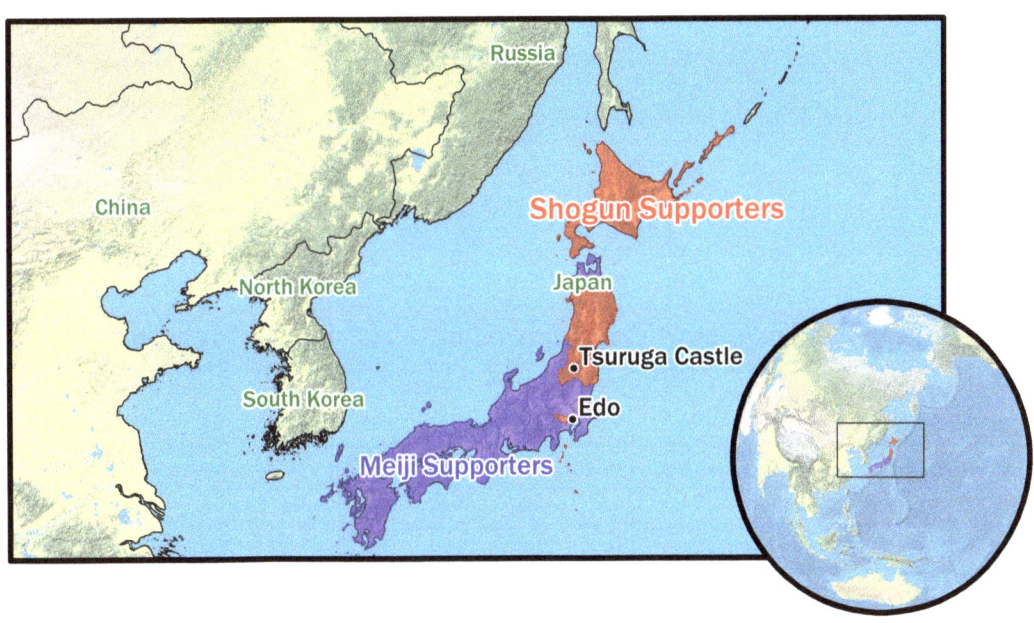

Nakano Takeko was born in Edo (now called Tokyo) in Japan. Her family were wealthy, and were of the samurai class. The samurai were highly regarded in Japanese society – they were specially trained warriors known for their discipline and courage.

Nakano was her family name, and Takeko her first name. (In some societies, the family name comes first as it is considered more important). Because of her family's samurai class, Takeko was well educated, and **she was taught martial arts, literature, and calligraphy** (special writing) as she grew up. She was inspired by stories of female warriors, particularly that of *Tomoe Gozen*.

Although **Japan had a long history of female samurai,** by Takeko's time, all samurai fighters were in decline – including the *onna-musha,* who were the female samurai. This was because Japan was modernising and warfare had changed greatly. Samurai fighters were no longer needed, and most people in the samurai class were now working in the government. However, some still followed the old traditions in learning to fight with samurai weapons and in the traditional ways. **Takeko was so adept** at the *naginata* (a long weapon, like a spear) that she was given the role of teaching younger students.

In 1868, civil war broke out – a clash now known as the *Boshin War.* Takeko, adept in martial arts training, **joined up to fight** – she fought for the ruling class, defending their hold on power from a faction who wanted to restore the Meiji emperor. **Takeko was the head of a whole corps of about twenty female warriors,** which included both her mother and her sister. She was just twenty-one years old!

The female army joined up with another force of 3,000 warriors, fighting alongside them against those who wanted the emperor back on the throne. Takeko and her corps fought bravely, but sadly her side lost the war and she was defeated.

The onna-musha were fully disbanded shortly after Takeko's time. **They had existed for almost 1,000 years.** The last known onna-musha fought in 1877. From then, women mostly stayed in their more traditional roles of being wives and mothers. However, in an annual autumn festival, young girls honour the memory of the onna-musha by wearing the *hakama* – traditional clothing, and special headbands.

Today, there is a monument to Nakano Takeko at the Hokai temple in Fukushima, Japan.

Nakano Takeko taught martial arts at Aizu Castle. During the Battle of Aizu she led a number of other onna-musha to defend the castle and fight against the forces of the Japanese Meiji Emperor.

INTERESTING FACTS:

There are many other famous onna-musha in Japanese history who are also celebrated. Niijima Yae was one of the last female samurai. After her time as an onna-musha, she became a nurse. She was also a scholar and she fought for women's rights.

Onna-musha wore the hakama, which was a long-legged wide trouser-skirt. Takeko wore red hakama. In Japan, the colour red had an important meaning: it meant bravery, strength, and energy.

Fun Quiz!

1. Who is your favourite heroine from this book, and why?
2. Which country were the *Onna-musha* from?
3. Can you name two of the leaders who fought against the Romans?
4. Khutulun was excellent at which sport?
5. What subjects did Hypatia teach in Alexandria?
6. What did Aethelflaed do to halt the Vikings?
7. Why is Al-Khansa famous?
8. Which other famous woman did Grace O'Malley meet with?
9. Which country was Njinga fighting against?
10. Where did Leif the Lucky and Freydis Eiriksdottir travel to?

And Finally....

There are many more awesome and interesting women through history to discover!

Who will **YOU** find?

www.ingramcontent.com/pod-product-compliance
Lightning Source LLC
Chambersburg PA
CBHW040042100526
44583CB00027BA/3254